VIRUS
OF THE
MIND

Also by Richard Brodie

GETTING PAST OK:
The Self-Help Book for People Who Don't Need Help
(available February 2010)

Hay House Titles of Related Interest

YOU CAN HEAL YOUR LIFE, the movie,
starring Louise L. Hay & Friends
(available as a 1-DVD program and an expanded 2-DVD set)
Watch the trailer at: **www.LouiseHayMovie.com**

THE SHIFT: the movie,
starring Wayne W. Dyer
(available as a 1-DVD program and an expanded 2-DVD set)
Watch the trailer at: **www.DyerMovie.com**

THE BIOLOGY OF BELIEF: Unleashing the Power of
Consciousness, Matter & Miracles, by Bruce H. Lipton, Ph.D.

FRACTAL TIME: The Secret of 2012 and a New World Age,
by Gregg Braden

THE LAST DROPOUT: Stop the Epidemic! by Bill Milliken

MIND PROGRAMMING: From Persuasion and
Brainwashing to Self-Help and Practical Metaphysics,
by Eldon Taylor (hardcover-with-CD)

EXCUSES BEGONE!: How to Change Lifelong,
Self-Defeating Thinking Habits, by Dr. Wayne W. Dyer

POWER vs. FORCE: The Hidden Determinants
of Human Behavior, by David R. Hawkins, M.D., Ph.D.

Please visit Hay House USA: **www.hayhouse.com**®
Hay House Australia: **www.hayhouse.com.au**
Hay House UK: **www.hayhouse.co.uk**
Hay House South Africa: **www.hayhouse.co.za**
Hay House India: **www.hayhouse.co.in**

Praise for *Virus of the Mind*

*"Brodie is infectious, indeed, but his
virus breeds truth. Those who ingest this book
are at great risk of seeing how things really are."*

— **Douglas Rushkoff**, the author of *Media Virus!*
and *Nothing Sacred*

*"This isn't a book—it's a mental adventure. **Virus of the Mind**
stimulates, educates, and awakens you to what really happens
to the things you see and hear. Buy it and study it."*

— **Jeffrey Gitomer**, the author of *The Sales Bible*

*"The true earmark of genius is taking a complex
concept and making it simple (for people like me) to
understand and, far more importantly, utilize. If the meme
truly is fundamental to behavior (child imitates child, child
imitates adult, world leader imitates world leader . . .), then
all of us need to spread memes with much greater intention—
and care! Brodie's humor makes this book a fun, absorbing,
educational, and at times controversial read. Pick up
this book, then give it to someone you love and
you will spread a truly valuable Virus!"*

— **Kevin Hogan, Psy.D.**, the co-author of *Irresistible
Attraction* and author of *The Psychology of Persuasion*

*"**Virus of the Mind** can do for memetics what Carl Sagan
has done for astronomy and astrophysics with **Cosmos**."*

— **Elan Moritz, Ph.D.**, director of the
Institute for Memetic Research

VIRUS
OF THE
MIND

The New Science of the Meme

Richard Brodie

HAY HOUSE, INC.
Carlsbad, California • New York City
London • Sydney • Johannesburg
Vancouver • Hong Kong • New Delhi

Published and distributed in the United States by: Hay House, Inc.: www.hay house.com • *Published and distributed in Australia by:* Hay House Australia Pty. Ltd.: www.hayhouse.com.au • *Published and distributed in the United Kingdom by:* Hay House UK, Ltd.: www.hayhouse.co.uk • *Published and distributed in the Republic of South Africa by:* Hay House SA (Pty), Ltd.: www.hayhouse.co.za • *Distributed in Canada by:* Raincoast: www.raincoast.com • *Published in India by:* Hay House Publishers India: www.hayhouse.co.in

Editorial supervision: Jill Kramer • *Design:* Tricia Breidenthal
Indexer: Richard Comfort

Previously published by Integral Press (ISBN: 0-9636001-2-5)

Library of Congress Cataloging-in-Publication Data

Brodie, Richard.
 Virus of the mind : the new science of the meme / Richard Brodie. -- 1st ed.
  p. cm.
 Includes index.
 Originally published: Seattle, Wash. : Integral Press, c1996.
 ISBN 978-1-4019-2468-3 (hardcover : alk. paper) 1. Social psychology. 2. Genetic psychology. 3. Contagion (Social psychology) 4. Public opinion. 5. Memetics. I. Title.
 HM626.B76 2009
 302--dc22

                                    2008046359

ISBN: 978-1-4019-2468-3

12 11 10 09   6 5 4 3
1st Hay House edition, May 2009
3rd Hay House edition, May 2009

Printed in the United States of America

For my mother,
Mary Ann Brodie,
who got me thinking . . .

CONTENTS

WARNING: This book contains a live mind virus. Do not read further unless you are willing to be infected. The infection may affect the way you think in subtle or not-so-subtle ways—or even turn your current worldview inside out.

INTRODUCTION

Crisis of the Mind

"What a waste it is to lose one's mind
or not to have a mind is very wasteful."

— Dan Quayle, mutating the memes in the United Negro
College Fund's motto, "A mind is a terrible thing to waste."

There *is* some good news in this book. So before I get into how
mind viruses are spreading wildly throughout the world—infecting
people with unwanted programming like the Michelangelo computer virus infects computers with self-destruct instructions—I'll
start with the good news. . . .

The good news is that the long-awaited scientific theory uni-
fying biology, psychology, and cognitive science is here. An inter-
disciplinary effort by scientists in all those fields over the last 20
years or so—really back to 1859 and Charles Darwin, if you like—
has produced a new science called *memetics*.

The science of memetics is based on evolution. Darwin's theory of the evolution of species by natural selection utterly transformed the field of biology. Scientists are now applying modern
evolutionary theory to the way the mind works, the way people
learn and grow, and the way culture progresses. In so doing, the
field of psychology will ultimately be as transformed by the scientists researching memetics as biology was by Darwin.

For those of us who yearn to understand ourselves, learning about memetics gives us a huge amount of satisfaction. I also believe that people who understand memetics will have an increasing advantage in life, especially in preventing themselves from being manipulated or taken advantage of. If you better understand how your mind works, you can better navigate through a world of increasingly subtle manipulation.

Now the bad news. . . . The bad news is that this book raises more questions than it answers. In particular, memetics has uncovered the existence of *viruses of the mind* but gives us few insights into what to do about them.

Viruses of the mind have been with us throughout history, but they are constantly evolving and changing. They are infectious pieces of our culture that spread rapidly throughout a population, altering people's thoughts and lives in their wake. Mind viruses include everything from the relatively harmless examples, such as miniskirts and slang phrases, to those that seriously derail people's lives, such as the cycle of unwed mothers on welfare, the Crips and Bloods youth gangs, and the Branch Davidian religious cult. When these pieces of culture are ones we like, there's no problem. However, just as the Michelangelo computer virus programs computers with instructions to destroy their data, viruses of the mind can program us to think and behave in ways that are destructive to our lives.

This is the most surprising and most profound insight from the science of memetics: your thoughts are not always your own original ideas. You catch thoughts—you get infected with them, both directly from other people and indirectly from viruses of the mind. People don't seem to like the idea that they aren't in control of their thoughts. The reluctance of people to even consider this notion is probably the main reason the scientific work done so far is not better known. As we'll see, ideas people don't like have a hard time catching on.

Further compounding the problem is that you don't immediately know whether the programming you get from a given mind virus is harmful or beneficial. Nobody ever joined a religious cult with the intention of getting brainwashed, moving to Guyana, and committing suicide. When the teenage Bill Gates caught the poker-playing mind virus at Harvard, was that harmful because it kept him from his studies? Or was it beneficial because it helped sway his decision to drop out, start Microsoft, and become a multi-billionaire?

Paradigm Shift

Every so often, the world of science experiences something called a *paradigm shift*. That happens when one of the basic, underlying assumptions we've been living with changes, such as when we shifted from looking at the universe as revolving around the earth to the earth revolving around the sun. Another shift occurred when Einstein discovered the relationships between space and time and between energy and matter. Each of these paradigm shifts took some time to penetrate the scientific community and even longer to become accepted by the general public.

> Viruses of the mind, and the whole science of memetics, represent a major paradigm shift in the science of the mind.

Because understanding this new science involves a significant change in the way people think about the mind and culture, it has been difficult for them to grasp. As with any paradigm shift, memetics doesn't fit into our existing way of looking at things, of understanding the world.

The trick to learning a new paradigm is to set aside your current one while you're learning rather than attempt to fit the new knowledge into your existing model. It won't fit! If you're willing to set aside your current thinking long enough to consider four concepts, some or all of which may be new to you, you'll be rewarded with an understanding of memetics. With that understanding, I hope, comes a call to action for anyone concerned with the future of human life.

— The first concept—the star of the show—is the **meme,** which I introduce in Chapter 1 and which plays a leading role throughout this book. The meme, which rhymes with "beam," is the basic building block of culture in the same way the gene is the basic building block of life. As I outline in Chapter 2, memes are not only the building blocks of culture on a large scale—making up countries, languages, and religions—but also on a small scale: memes are the building blocks of your mind, the programming of your mental "computer."

— Second is the concept of **virus.** It's well known that viruses exist in biology and in the world of computers. Now we'll see how they show up in the world of mind and culture, the world of memetics. In Chapter 3, I'll draw parallels between the three different universes that viruses live in to show what we can expect from mind viruses in the future.

— The third concept that contributes to this paradigm shift is **evolution.** Evolution is one of those words that many people use, thinking they are talking about the same thing but really having different ideas of what it is and means. I'll discuss scientists' most current theory of evolution in Chapter 4 and how it applies to memes in Chapter 5.

— The fourth concept necessary to understanding mind viruses is the new science of **evolutionary psychology.** This field examines the biases and mechanisms of our minds that evolved to support our survival and reproduction. Some of these biases take the form of psychological *buttons* that can be pushed to penetrate our mental defenses. I called this part of the book "Crisis of the Mind" rather than simply "Introduction" because the former pushes more buttons: it attracts more attention, and more people will read it. I called this book *Virus of the Mind* rather than *Introduction to Memetics* for the same reason.

Currently a controversial topic, evolutionary psychology explores and explains many of the stereotypical differences between men and women, especially in the realm of mating behavior. Chapter 6 is about the mating part of evolutionary psychology; Chapter 7 covers the survival aspect.

Memetics builds on these four conceptual blocks to form a new paradigm of how culture evolved and is evolving. It illuminates a major decision point for humanity:

> Will we allow natural selection to evolve us randomly, without regard for our happiness, satisfaction, or spirit? Or will we seize the reins of our own evolution and pick a direction for ourselves?

Memetics gives us the knowledge and power to direct our own evolution more than we've done at any time in history. Now that we have that power, what will we do with it?

A Threat to Humanity

A mind virus is not spread by sneezing, like the flu, or by sex, like AIDS. It's not a physical thing. Mind viruses are spread by something as simple as communicating. I discuss the ways we get programmed by mind viruses in Chapter 8. In a way, mind viruses are the price of one of the freedoms most dear to us: freedom of speech. The more freedom there is to put forth any communication, the more welcoming the environment for mind viruses.

Some mind viruses arise spontaneously, as I discuss in Chapters 9 and 10; some are created intentionally, as I cover in Chapter 11. But all of them share one thing in common:

> Once created, a virus of the mind gains a life *independent* of its creator and evolves quickly to infect as many people as possible.

Viruses of the mind are not some far-off future worry like the sun burning out or the earth being hit by a comet. They are here with us now—have been with us since before recorded history— and they are evolving to become better and better at their job of infecting us. We are being infected in some new ways (television, popular music, sales techniques), but also in very ancient ways (education, religious teachings, even talking to our closest friends). Our parents unwittingly infected us when we were kids. If you have children, chances are that you are spreading the viruses to them every day.

Read a newspaper? Catch a mind virus. Listen to the radio? Catch a mind virus. Hang out with your friends and shoot the breeze about nothing in particular? Catch one mind virus after another. If your life isn't going the way you would like, you can bet mind viruses are playing a large part. Having relationship problems? Mind viruses take over parts of your brain and divert you from what would give you long-term happiness. Having trouble in your job or career? Mind viruses cloud your future and steer you along a career path that supports *their* agenda, not *your* quality of life.

Cult religions are springing up everywhere, the result of more and more powerful mind viruses. These cults take control of people's minds and make members engage in bizarre behavior, ranging from odd rituals to mass suicide. If you think you're immune, remember: nobody ever set out intentionally to join a cult and have their mind taken over. It's the work of tricky and pernicious mind viruses. And once the founder of the cult starts the process, the virus of the mind takes on a life of its own.

Because of mass media and direct elections, the U.S. and other governments are becoming more and more subject to infection by mind viruses. A politician today cannot be elected without coming up with an effective image that pushes people's buttons and gets the votes. "We're having a crisis, and only I can fix it," they say, or "Those other guys have caused all these problems; surely any change is better than what we've got!" Politicians' well-crafted images are hooks into some of the most elaborate and pervasive mind viruses infecting society today.

What brand of soft drink do you buy? The ones that sell the most cost twice as much as unadvertised store brands. The extra money goes into television advertising, sending out the spores of ever-more-penetrating mind viruses that take control of your mind and coerce you to push your shopping cart over to their shelf. Successfully programming your mind to believe that you prefer that brand, advertising agencies are among the most brazen and calculating of the mind-virus instigators.

The unchecked spread of mind viruses shows up most alarmingly in the state of our children today. Starting with the inner cities and quickly spreading, the mind viruses infecting many kids are pushing them into hopelessness, single motherhood, and gang warfare. Many young people seem to be losing their sense of values and taking off in some very unsettling directions. Chapter 12 discusses the possibility of disinfection for our children and ourselves.

My Agenda

Let me tell you right now—I have an agenda in writing this book, and that is to make a difference in people's lives. Some of the content found herein *could* be used for self-improvement. You might not expect a book about science to include ideas from the self-development field, but the science of memetics deals with the mind, with people's lives. Understanding memetics can naturally help increase the quality of people's lives.

In the first place, I would never have written this book—or my first one, *Getting Past OK*—if I had not intentionally disinfected myself of many of the memes that I got as I grew up and then reprogrammed myself with new memes. What new memes would you choose to reprogram yourself with, given the chance? That's entirely up to you. I had no idea what that even *meant* when I started this research. Now that I do, I choose to program myself with memes that support my values in life rather than ones that support the agendas of viruses of the mind. You can do that or something different. But you won't have the option to do anything like that unless you understand memetics.

The reason I'm writing this book is that I really *enjoy* making a difference in people's lives. I believe that knowledge of memetics is important, so I'm spreading the word. I'm not just writing this book as an intellectual exercise. Although *Virus of the Mind* is *about* science, it's obviously not a scientific text. It's designed with an intention, and that is to consciously spread the new paradigm of memetics because I think it's of value.

> Consciously spreading ideas you consider important is one way to combat mind viruses.

Have you ever wondered why life seems so complicated today—more complicated and stressful year after year? One reason is the ever-evolving army of mind viruses, taking over a greater and greater portion of your mind, diverting you from your pursuit of happiness and due to have an even greater effect on the next generation.

Ever wonder why, with greater and greater progress and technology, life doesn't seem to get simpler, but just the reverse? Every time you're exposed to a new virus of the mind, your mind takes on just a little more stress, a little more confusion.

People are flocking to everything from psychotherapy to the New Age movement to try to relieve the crushing burden of stress. Doctors are more and more certain that excess stress is our number one killer, but experts disagree on what causes stress and how to cure it. The medical community talked of stressed-out "type A" and laid-back "type B" personalities, with no clear idea of what caused someone to have one or the other. And even the "type B's" had stress-related symptoms at times. The new science of memetics gives much insight into the problem of stress.

> Taking over bits of your mind and pulling you in different directions, mind viruses distract you from what's most important to you in life and cause confusion, stress, and even despair.

Mind viruses infect your mind, programming you with directions that point you away from where you want to go. Since this happens unconsciously, all you're aware of is that as you grow older, life becomes more stressful, less fun, more of a drag, and less meaningful. You may feel your motivation slipping away. You may get less excited about things than you used to. These are some of the effects of infection by a virus of the mind, an infection you can't avoid entirely short of living in complete isolation from birth.

You *can,* however, begin to disinfect yourself. My hope is that the understanding you gain from this book will be a big first step in that disinfection. But it takes a bit of effort to teach yourself a new paradigm.

Birth of a New Paradigm

It's always been hard for scientists to communicate their ideas to the general public. Science, by its very nature, is an artificial selection of ideas based on rigorous testing of their usefulness *rather than on people's gut feelings.* As such, new scientific ideas tend to rub people the wrong way at first and produce predictable reactions. When Charles Darwin first proposed his theories on natural selection in 1859, there were several stages of public reaction—ones that any revolutionary new scientific idea seems to go through before becoming accepted:

1. Complacency/Marginalization. At first, the new theory is seen as an off-the-wall idea: quaint, but not a serious threat to the dominant worldview—perhaps a simple variant of some already-known theory. Memetics is graduating from this stage to the next as I write this. Editors of *The New York Times Magazine* of January 22, 1995, picked up on the growing use of the word *meme* and mildly attempted to marginalize it: "A skeptic might wonder what the notion of a meme adds to the paradigm of cultural evolution. Perhaps there is nothing new under the sun." By the end of this book, you will discover that rather than adding to the existing paradigm of cultural evolution, memetics itself is a new and more powerful paradigm.

2. Ridicule. Complacency fades as the new idea refuses to die, resulting in ridicule by people who clearly and laughingly see that it's inconsistent with something they hold to be true. In Darwin's case, contemporaries laughed at the naturalist's inability to see the necessity of a Supreme Designer doing the selecting. Darwin was frustrated by his seeming inability to communicate this new paradigm. Similar ridicule of memetics is seen from time to time in the few places where this topic is discussed.

3. Criticism. As the new idea gains acceptance, people who have held conflicting worldviews for some time, or who have their reputation invested in old paradigms, take off their gloves. Darwinism is still being attacked today by creationists, who believe it conflicts with their Truth. It's possible that this book will touch off serious criticism of memetics. If it does, we shouldn't worry; it's the nature of a paradigm shift.

4. Acceptance. Finally, enough people make the leap to the new paradigm that it gains psychological as well as intellectual acceptance. Those who understand the new ideas are no longer as alone and unloved as Columbus among the flat-Earth believers. The new world agrees on the new paradigm. Peer pressure starts to work for it rather than against it. It begins to be taught in elementary schools. Scientists can move on to their next challenge.

Our minds, it seems, are not well equipped to understand how they themselves work. You, in fact, may at first be very confused or distracted, or suddenly get tired, as you read this; you may even become angry just from reading these words. Although right now you may think that this statement is absurd, those feelings and symptoms are actually the defense mechanisms of mind viruses.

They have evolved to be very protective of the parts of your mind that they've stolen, and any attempts to cleanse yourself of them can trigger reactions.

If you experience one or more of these reactions while reading this book, don't worry: the reaction will pass if you ride it out. If you do, you'll be rewarded with a powerful tool for your future . . . and the future of humanity.

CHAPTER ONE

MEMES

"There are no whole truths; all truths
are half-truths. It is trying to treat them
as whole truths that plays the devil."

— Alfred North Whitehead

I first heard the word *meme* several years ago during a typical hard-nosed political discussion in the Microsoft cafeteria. It wasn't often in those days that I heard a new word while dining. I probably had enough arrogance to think that, being fairly well-read and having attended Harvard for three and a half years, I had already learned most words likely to be used in a cafeteria setting.

I was lunching with Charles Simonyi and Greg Kusnick, two of my most esteemed colleagues at Microsoft. Having lunch with brilliant and well-educated men of this sort was always my secret reason for working at Microsoft. Charles, in fact, hired me to work there in 1981 and assigned me to write the first version of Microsoft Word a year later. (That turned out well. I now realize Word had good memes.)

We were talking about politics and government, about why pork-barrel projects continued to get funded, about why ineffective or corrupt politicians continued to get elected. Were voters just stupid? (A common meme at Microsoft was that if something didn't get done the way it ought to, there was a good chance it was because somebody was just stupid.) Charles replied, with his Hungarian accent and customary pith, through bites of his usual Caesar salad, no anchovies, add red peppers:

"Good memes."

"*Gesundheit!*" I said.

"No, goood meemes," Charles reiterated.

"Good *what?*" I asked insistently.

"Meemes, *meeeeemes!*" Charles rebutted.

"Memes," chimed in Kusnick.

"You're kidding!" said Charles, incredulous. "You have never heard of memes?"

"You don't know about memes?" chimed in Kusnick.

"Memes?" I repeated, starting to sound like a mooing cow, with about as much to contribute to this conversation. "What's a meme?"

"It's like Beethoven's Fifth Symphony," Charles ventured.

Kusnick demurred: "Wait a minute—I disagree with that. I'm not sure Beethoven's Fifth Symphony is a meme. It may *have* good memes, but it's not *a* meme."

Charles wrinkled his brow to ponder this challenge to his position. "Well—mumble." He actually *said* "mumble." That's a meme (or is it?) he picked up from his days at Xerox Palo Alto Research Center (PARC). It served the function of preventing anyone else from using up the conversational bandwidth (that is, talking) while he was audibly considering what to say next.

"Okay, you're right," Charles conceded. "Beethoven's Fifth Symphony isn't a meme. *Ta-ta-ta-TUM* is the meme."

Kusnick said, "No, I don't even think *ta-ta-ta-TUM* is a meme. Or if it is, it's a meme in a very limited sense of the word. But it's a poor example."

"What's a good example?" I piped up, getting curiouser and curiouser.

"Well," said Kusnick, "I guess if you were to go around humming *ta-ta-ta-TUM,* that would be a good meme. But I don't think that's what Charles is talking about. The fact that there are millions of copies of Beethoven's Fifth Symphony on record albums and CDs doesn't make it a good meme."

"Oh, I beg to differ," said Charles.

Kusnick said, "Hmm. So you're saying a library is just a book's way of making another book." Before I had a chance to analyze *that* pithy remark, he went on: "See, I think—and this may be a philosophical point—that memes have to do with human beings. So if you make a bunch of photocopies* of a document, that doesn't give it good memes. But if you hand them out and people start memorizing them and reciting them, then it's a good meme."

Charles's mind processed this thought, an awesome sight to behold. "Well, mumble. Okay. Good point."

"Thank you."

No one said anything for a few seconds, and I began to panic as I realized that they thought they were done with the conversation and I still didn't know what a meme was. I was getting that it had something to do with information, and I thought I'd float a trial balloon.

"So," I said, "a meme is any information?"

Charles and Kusnick opened their mouths simultaneously, and Kusnick said, "May I? Thank you. A meme is anything that gets imitated. It's the basic unit of imitation."

"So a yawn would be a meme," I ventured.

"Hmm. No. Well, yes. I don't know. That's a tricky one. Heh-heh-heh."

"Hoh-hoh-hoh," chuckled Charles. "You got caught by your own trap."

"No, I didn't," said Kusnick. "It's just that a yawn is behavior, and I think memes are thoughts."

---

*Kusnick, Charles, and I all worked at Xerox in the late '70s. The reason Kusnick is always called by his last name is that there were two other Gregs working with Charles at that time. The distinctive sound of Charles poking his head out into the hall calling "Kusnick!" was a catchy meme. Anyway, as part of the Xerox employee orientation/indoctrination, we were taught to never use the corporate trademark as a generic word for "photocopy." Both of those memes stayed with us.

"Come on!" exclaimed Charles. "You are asking the wrong question! Who cares if a yawn is a meme or not?! The right question is, 'What are the interesting memes?'"

"Exactly," chimed in Kusnick.

"What are the interesting memes?" I asked, always good at following instructions.

"Good question," affirmed Charles.

I spent much of the next two years looking for answers to that question.

Memes and Memetics

The meme is the secret code of human behavior, a Rosetta stone finally giving us the key to understanding religion, politics, psychology, and cultural evolution. That key, though, also unlocks Pandora's box, opening up such sophisticated new techniques for mass manipulation that we may soon look on today's manipulative TV commercials, political speeches, and televangelists as fond remembrances of the good old days.

The word *meme* was coined by Oxford biologist Richard Dawkins in his 1976 book *The Selfish Gene.* Since then it has been tossed about by Dawkins and other evolutionary biologists, psychologists such as Henry Plotkin, and cognitive scientists such as Douglas Hofstadter and Daniel Dennett in an effort to flesh out the biological, psychological, and philosophical implications of this new model of consciousness and thought.*

The meme has a central place in the paradigm shift that's currently taking place in the science of life and culture. In the new paradigm, we look at cultural evolution from the point of view of the meme, rather than the point of view of an individual or society.

Why bother to look at life in this new, upsetting, inside-out way? Well, for the same reason explorers started to look at the earth as round instead of flat, and the same reason astronomers

---

*See the Recommended Reading section at the back of the book for references to the work of these scientists.

4

stopped looking at the universe as if it revolved around the earth: it makes a lot more sense, and you can get more exciting things accomplished when you find a better model for explaining the way the world works. Such a model is the theory of the meme, or *memetics*.

Memetics is the study of the workings of memes: how they interact, replicate, and evolve.

The science of memetics is the mind universe's analogue to *genetics*, which studies the same things about genes in the biological universe.

Defining the Meme

It's not so easy to answer even the obvious question, "What is a meme?" If you ask a biologist, the answer is likely to be along the lines of Dawkins's original definition:

Biological Definition of <u>Meme</u> (from Dawkins)

The *meme* is the basic unit of cultural transmission, or imitation.

According to this definition, everything we call "culture" is composed of atomlike memes, which compete with one another. These memes spread by being passed from mind to mind in the same way genes spread by being passed down through sperm and egg. The memes that win this competition—those that are successful at penetrating the most minds—are the ones responsible for the activities and creations that constitute present-day culture.

The most interesting memes to a biologist have to do with behavior. Dawkins's original examples of memes were:

. . . tunes, ideas, catch-phrases, clothes fashions, ways of making pots or of building arches.

According to the biological definition, women wear long skirts one year, then a new short-skirt meme catches on for whatever reason, and now women wear short skirts. Popular songs compete for the Top 40, each a meme or perhaps a bundle of memes. Then people start humming the catchy tunes, spreading those memes even further. Engineers build bridges on the cantilever principle; then the suspension bridge is invented and its meme spreads quickly to become the new state of the art in bridge building.

This biological definition is kind of satisfying, because it gives us a way to reduce all of culture to manageable pieces and start to label them and see how they interact and evolve. Frustratingly, though, it doesn't lend much insight into the question of *why* certain memes spread and others don't. So let's put that definition on hold for a moment and look at some other points of view.

A Psychological Definition

If a psychologist were asked what a meme is, he would give a slightly different answer, one that illuminates more the workings of the mind than the components of behavior. Here is psychologist Henry Plotkin's definition of *meme:*

Psychological Definition of <u>Meme</u> (from Plotkin)

A *meme* is the unit of cultural heredity analogous to the gene. It is the internal representation of knowledge.

This definition stresses the analogy to genes, which are tiny chemical patterns living on strands of DNA. As those tiny DNA patterns cause all kinds of external effects—eye and hair color, blood type, even whether you grow up to be a human or a golden retriever—the memes in your head cause behavioral effects. Likening your mind to a computer, memes are the software part of your programming; the brain and central nervous system, produced by your genes, are the hardware part.

The memes in this definition don't live in the external trappings of culture, but in the mind. After all, it is in each individual's mind where the competition for memes takes place. According to this definition, a woman might have in mind a meme like *It's good to be aware of the current fashion;* another meme, *Women who dress fashionably get ahead;* and a third meme, *I want to get ahead.* Wearing short skirts when they become fashionable is a behavior that results from having all these memes working together in her mind. If there are enough women who have these supporting memes in their minds, all it would take would be one more meme—*Short skirts are fashionable*—to cause a proliferation of raised hemlines.

Bridge-building methods evolve because of memes. An engineer might be programmed with memes such as *Suspension bridges are the most efficient for this kind of job; Engineers who do a good job get their bosses' approval;* and *Getting the approval of my boss is important.* Without any of these three, the engineer might not build a suspension bridge. All three memes acting together cause something to get built out in the world. Of course, the engineer works with other engineers, construction workers, teamsters, and so on, all behaving as directed by their memes.

Under this definition, memes are to a human's behavior what our genes are to our bodies: internal representations of knowledge that result in outward effects on the world. Genes are hidden, internal pieces of information stored in an embryo that *result,* with the influence of its environment, in the flesh and blood of the developed organism. Memes are hidden, internal representations of knowledge that *result,* again along with environmental influence, in external behavior and the production of cultural artifacts such as skirts and bridges. If I look around and see short skirts, that might cause the production of a meme in my mind such as *Short skirts are in fashion.* But the meme is in my mind, not on Meg Ryan's body.

If someone is having difficulties in life, a memetic psychologist might explore what memes the patient has that are producing the undesirable results. Once discovered, those memes could be changed.*

This way of looking at memes is useful for understanding how people work. However, it still has some problems as a complete theory of the evolution of knowledge. It centers around the human mind, and not all knowledge in the world is stored in people's minds. As people interact with other forms of knowledge—geography, the genetic knowledge contained in each organism's DNA, the astronomical knowledge of the universe—how does that affect culture and behavior?

A Cognitive Definition

We can eliminate ourselves from the picture entirely, then, and look at an even more abstract definition of *meme*. This one is from cognitive scientist and philosopher Daniel Dennett:

> ### Cognitive Definition of <u>Meme</u> (from Dennett)
>
> A *meme* is an idea, the kind of complex idea that forms itself into a distinct memorable unit. It is spread by *vehicles* that are physical manifestations of the meme.

---

*This is in fact close to what goes on in the practice of cognitive therapy, pioneered by psychologist Albert Ellis and psychiatrist Aaron Beck in the 1950s. Cognitive therapists theorize that unwanted mental states such as depression are the result of incorrect thinking ("cognition") about life and the world. Since the patient is living with an inaccurate model of reality, naturally he or she has difficulty succeeding in life. The cognitive therapist interviews the patient and methodically uncovers and "corrects" illogical or inaccurate beliefs, eventually leaving the patient with a better working model of how to get along in life and therefore a feeling of well-being.

As Dennett says:

> A wagon with spoked wheels carries not only grain or freight from place to place; it carries the brilliant idea of a wagon with spoked wheels from mind to mind.

Now *this* definition really gives you a meme's-eye view of the universe. Notice the phrase "forms itself." Well, we know ideas don't *form themselves* any more than spoons get up and dance on the table. This definition is a scientific model—and as we have seen, there are many such models possible just surrounding the term *meme*. Using the phrase "forms itself" is a trick to get us to look at things from a meme's point of view. You notice interesting things when you look at a specific meme and see what happens around it: how it spreads, mutates, or dies.

Someone whose mind carried the *spoked wheel* meme might build a wagon with spoked wheels. Someone else would see the wagon, "catch" the *spoked wheel* meme, and build another wagon. The process would then repeat itself indefinitely. Unlike the biological definition, this view of memes places them in the realm of the unseen—software of the mind, ready to produce results in the physical world that then carry their own seeds to other human beings.

The cognitive definition gives us license to take out a magnifying glass and follow around a specific meme like a private investigator—watching to see how infection with it affects people's behavior; noticing how people spread it; comparing it with competing memes, like the suspension bridge with the cantilever—to see what properties it has that make it occupy more or fewer minds than its rivals.

One potential pitfall with this definition is the use of the term *vehicles*. The distinction of a meme-carrying vehicle is not as clear-cut as in biology, where organisms are vehicles for the spread of DNA. Not all meme transmission is as simple as imitating a catchy tune or noticing a spoked wheel.

The Adventures of Eggbert

Once someone builds a spoked wheel or makes a recording of Beethoven's Fifth Symphony, those physical objects serve as vehicles to spread memes—in this case, the *spoked wheel* meme and the *ta-ta-ta-TUM* meme—indirectly to new minds.

If memes are our internal programming, we can draw on decades of research in psychology to look at how we get programmed—how memes get transmitted into our minds. Once programmed, we behave in complex ways that spread memes indirectly.

So while it may sometimes be illuminating to use the term *vehicle* to describe behavior or an artifact that tends to infect people with a meme, more often the existence of a meme will trigger a Rube Goldberg–like sequence of actions that only indirectly causes spreading of the meme. The wagon wheel and the commercial advertising on TV programs are the exceptions as meme-spreading vehicles; the rule is more complex.

A Working Definition

We want a definition of *meme* that gives us access to understanding cultural evolution, as in the biological definition. But we want to be clear that memes are internal representations, as in the psychological definition. And we want to look at memes as ideas—as our software, our own internal programming—that produce an effect on the outside world, as in the cognitive definition. The result is the definition I use in this book, a definition similar to the one Dawkins adopted in his 1982 book *The Extended Phenotype:*

Definition of Meme

A *meme* is a unit of information in a mind whose existence influences events such that more copies of itself get created in other minds.

Now, with this definition, we can answer the questions I asked Charles Simonyi and Greg Kusnick back at Microsoft. *Is a yawn a meme?* No, a yawn is behavior and, as far as I know, has nothing to do with an internal representation of any information. While it appears to be self-replicating, it's more like an unreliable radio relay: see a yawn, emit a yawn, maybe. It's not influencing events such that more copies of information get created. People yawn when they see others do so, but their internal state hasn't changed to make them more likely to yawn in the future, or to do anything that I am aware of.

How about *ta-ta-ta-TUM*, the famous motif from Beethoven's Fifth Symphony? As it's stored in my brain, Charles's, and Kusnick's, it is a meme. I've just infected you with a copy of it. If you hear the music, or hear anyone talk about Beethoven's Fifth in the next few days, you'll have no choice but to associate it with this discussion. If you then start up a conversation and say, "Hey, that's odd! I just read about *ta-ta-ta-TUM* in this book *Virus of the Mind*, and do you know it's a meme?" you will be spreading some of the memes from this book that you're already infected with.

Metamemes!

This book is a collection of ideas about memes. When you read and understand it, you'll have memes about memes in your head—metamemes! If you write a book about memes, tell someone else about memetics, or lend your copy of *Virus of the Mind* to someone who reads and understands it, then the metamemes in your mind will have self-replicated.

One metameme I want to stress is that everything in these pages is, as Whitehead admonishes in the quote that begins this chapter, a half-truth. Now that's not an indictment of this book; I, and Whitehead, would say the same about every other science book. My point is, memetics is a scientific model. It's one way of looking at things. It's looking at ideas—memes—as distinct entities in competition for a share of your mind and a share of everyone else's. When those ideas are harmful ones and they become part of an infectious mind virus, understanding this model can show you how to combat the infection.

> I'm *not* saying this is the Truth.* I'm *not* saying this is what Really Happens. I'm *not* saying this is the Only Way or the Right Way to look at the mind.

A neuroscientist would say what is *really* happening when an idea forms in your mind is that a complex web of electrochemical changes is occurring in various parts of the brain; this person might even point out which parts those are and show experimental evidence that patients with brain damage in those areas are unable to have that meme in their minds. This is completely valid; it's just not what this book is about. It's not memetics.

A psychologist would say what is happening is that there are certain unfulfilled drives, competing instincts, past traumas, and so on that contribute to the ideas people think and speak. Again, this is a perfectly valid model, but it's not what this book is about; it's not memetics.

In the last few years, physics has collided with philosophy. We now understand so much about quantum physics—the physics of particles smaller than atoms—that we realize it's impossible to separate reality from the observer of reality. We were so sure all matter was composed of atoms. Then we got so excited when we discovered atoms were themselves made up of protons, neutrons, and electrons. It was a little disturbing when we found that there seemed to be lots of empty space inside the atoms, but those protons and neutrons looked like the basic units of matter: more solid than a rock.

Today we've sliced up even the proton and neutron. Physicists have equations that describe the behavior of the components of these subatomic particles. The trouble is, they don't really seem to behave like matter. They don't quite behave like energy, though, either. And to top it off, the famous uncertainty principle of Werner Heisenberg states that it's impossible to measure these things further without actually changing them. It's as if they don't really

---

*Throughout this book I use *Truth* or *True* with a capital *T* when referring to the concept of absolute, eternal truth—a concept that frequently leads to Trouble.

exist in a particular time and place until we attempt to measure them.

What all this points out is the memetic nature of everything we call reality. All of our labels for things are memes, not Truth. The idea of atoms is a meme, invented in ancient Greece. The idea of subatomic particles and those complex formulas that describe them—quantum physics—is a newer set of memes.

If your model of reality, as the Greeks believed, was that there were four elements—*earth, air, fire,* and *water*—you might spend a lot of time trying to convert lead into gold. If your model of reality is that we have dozens of elements made of immutable and indivisible atoms, you won't waste that time. And if your model of reality is that those atoms can be split, you have research leading to atomic energy and the Bomb. The way you describe reality—the memes you have that label things—makes a big difference in life.

That's why the metamemes in this book are important. You could easily go through life without any of these ideas about memetics, just as the Greeks went through life not knowing about the elements of the periodic table. But knowledge of elements has given us everything from steel to computer chips. Likewise, knowledge of memetics opens up enormous possibilities for understanding many of the problems we now consider impossible: ending world hunger, preventing human-rights abuses, and giving each child an opportunity for education and the pursuit of happiness.

These social issues that just won't seem to go away—these persistent, infectious cultural plagues—are universally considered undesirable, but they keep spreading. Memetics identifies these problems as viruses of the mind, giving us, perhaps for the first time, tools powerful enough to deal with them.

"Good Memes" and Mind Viruses

When Charles Simonyi used the succinct explanation "good memes" to explain why we kept electing ineffective politicians, he didn't mean that ineffectiveness was a good idea. He meant that there were memes present in people's minds that influenced them to vote for those candidates, and that those memes, for whatever reason, were *good at spreading*.

> If I talk about a *good meme* or a *successful meme*, I'm talking about an idea or belief that spreads easily throughout the population, not necessarily what we think of as a "good idea."

Some memes spread directly from mind to mind. Yelling "Fire!" in a crowded theater does a great job of spreading that meme from mind to mind quickly. Some spread more indirectly. A mother, not wanting to perpetuate the unhappy experience she had when *her* mother raised her with iron discipline, may react by raising her daughter with a very loose rein—a meme for the opposite child-rearing strategy. The granddaughter, in turn, may react to her unhappy experience of the loose rein by resuming Grandmother's iron hand. The *iron hand* meme got transmitted indirectly.*

Memes can spread in ways that are easy to understand, like those examples, or they can spread through a complicated chain of cause and effect, almost randomly, chaotically. But out of the chaos occasionally arises a stable web of cause and effect: *something* goes on in the world that infects people with certain memes, and those memes eventually influence their hosts' behavior in such a way that the *something* gets repeated and/or spread. That *something* is a virus of the mind.

Nazi beliefs spread quickly throughout Hitler's Germany because a virus of the mind was unleashed that successfully infected people with those memes—not because they were "good ideas" in any other sense. In fact, Nazism was a pathological virus of the mind—a classic case of an epidemic thought-infection producing horrifying atrocities as a result of the behavior of people infected with its memes.

---

*But perhaps the *I don't want to be like my mother* meme was passed on directly.

> A virus of the mind is something out in the world that infects people with memes. Those memes, in turn, influence the infected people's behavior so that they help perpetuate and spread the virus.

I know the word *something* is about as vague as you can get, and I promise I'll cover in detail what kinds of memes, and what kinds of mind viruses, are good at spreading before the end of the book. For now I'll just assert that the memes that spread successfully are *not* necessarily the ones that maximize people's quality of life—in fact, they're often harmful. And the memes that mind viruses infect you with to perpetuate themselves range from distracting to disastrous.

The science of memetics, like all sciences, is a set of memes designed to give you access to and power over some aspect of the universe. Remember, I didn't say, "Memetics is the way the universe actually works," or "We now know memetics is the Truth about the functioning of the human mind." It's not the Truth; it's a model, like all sciences—like all memes. Once you start believing memes are True, you lose your power to pick and choose which memes you're programmed with, and you become more subject to infection by mind viruses.

> The most interesting thing about memes is not whether they're true or false; it's that they are the building blocks of your mind.

The aspect of the universe that memetics gives you access to is a particularly interesting one: what causes you and everyone else to think and behave as they do. The purpose of this book is to teach you—infect you with—the set of memes called memetics. There's a lot you can do with that knowledge, from improving your mental fitness to perhaps creating a new golden age for humanity. To begin with, let's look at how memes work to form your mind and influence your behavior.

CHAPTER TWO

MIND AND BEHAVIOR

*"Every man's work, whether it be literature or
music or pictures or architecture or anything
else, is always a portrait of himself."*

— Samuel Butler

Memes spread by influencing people's minds, and thus their behavior, so that eventually someone else gets infected with the meme. If a meme is in your mind, it can greatly or subtly influence your behavior.

In this book, I'm going to write as though *all* your behavior is dictated by a combination of the instructions in your DNA and the mental programming you acquired as you grew up: your genes and your memes. Some people believe there's a third factor in there: a soul, a spirit, a little "me! me! me!" demanding recognition as something more than machinery. This "me!" factor is, according to your beliefs, either a divinely injected spark or simply a biological trait like an opposable thumb or a high IQ: some combination of genes and memes. Fortunately, we don't have to resolve that particular philosophical issue right here, since either belief works fine for understanding memetics and this book.

Instincts and Programming

There are certain tendencies you have because you are a product of nature. These tendencies support your survival and reproduction. They are things like your sex drive and your desire to breathe, eat, sleep, and so forth. Scientists have a number of different names for different brands of these tendencies, but I'm just going to lump them all together under the term *instincts*.

> Unfortunately, human instincts evolved to support our survival a long time ago and didn't take into account the kind of world we live in today.

In modern times, those prehistoric instincts often don't work any better than a deer's instinct to freeze in the face of oncoming headlights. Fortunately, we have conscious minds that we can use to override our instincts and propel us in the direction of our pursuit of happiness. So as you read the next few chapters, which outline in painful detail just how poorly adapted we are to modern life, remember: instincts are just instincts; tendencies are just tendencies. Knowing what they are gives you more power to consciously override them if you choose.

The study of how your instincts evolved is called *evolutionary psychology,* covered in Chapters 6 and 7. It's important to understand human instincts, because they have a great influence on the evolution of memes. The memes that appeal to people's instincts are more likely to replicate and spread throughout the population than the ones that don't.

Everything you do that is not instinctual is the result of *programming.* You are programmed by memes. If you went to college, you probably did so to get educated, which is to say, to get programmed with a set of memes that would support your success in life. Having been to college, you have thoughts and behaviors you wouldn't have had if you were just going on instinct.

Most memes that people are programmed with are acquired without any conscious intent; they just infect you and there you are, living your life by their programming. Such programming includes:

- Your religious (or atheistic) upbringing

- The example your parents set of how relationships work, or don't

- The TV shows and commercials you've watched

In Chapter 8, I'll cover the ways in which we get programmed—how programming, especially unwanted programming, gets into our minds. First, though, let's look at the nature of that programming. Let's look at the nature of memes.

What kinds of memes are there? I've divided memes into three classes: *distinctions,* knives used to slice up reality; *strategies,* beliefs about which causes will produce which effects; and *associations,* attitudes about everything in life. Each class of meme works to program you in a different way. I'll explain why I chose these three classes in Chapter 5, where we look at the origins of memes, but this division into classes is simply a convenience and certainly not True with a captial *T.*

Distinction-memes

The universe is full of stuff. However, anything we say about that stuff is purely a concept—a set of memes—invented by human beings. All concepts are composed of memes. For instance, the United States are only states because we have invented 50 distinctions—memes—carving out that territory. Alabama isn't a reality; it's just there because we say so, because we are programmed with a meme for Alabama. If we didn't have an Alabama meme, that land would just be more dirt.

Likewise, the earth is simply a distinction—a meme—we invented because it was convenient to put edges around the place we live in order to distinguish it from the rest of the universe. To the universe, it's all just stuff. You may say, "But there really *are* edges! There's where the dirt ends and the atmosphere begins, or where the atmosphere gives way to outer space!" Really? *Dirt, atmosphere, outer space*—they're all memes. If you think dirt is really dirt, not a meme we invented for our convenience, then all you'll ever have is dirt. If you see that it's a meme, not the Truth, you open up the possibility of other memes to talk about the same thing: elements, crystals, subatomic particles. Remember that viewed through an electron microscope, it's all mostly empty space!

How about this one: *you* are simply a distinction—a meme— invented because it was convenient to talk about the parts of the universe that feel pain when hit with a hammer. To the universe, there's no *you* . . . or human beings or giraffes or solar systems or galaxies. All those are human-invented distinctions. They are all memes.

Now one more point: everything I just said about the distinction between objective reality and concepts . . . is a concept. It's a meme. To the universe, there's no such thing as a concept. I just drew this distinction because it was convenient to use when we're talking about memetics.

> Distinctions are one kind of meme. They are ways of carving up the world by categorizing or labeling things.

When you create a distinction, you gain access to some things and lose access to others. It's useful to be conscious of what distinction-memes you're programmed with and to know that all the distinctions you draw are human invented and not reality.

Distinctions, as I just mentioned, are one kind of meme that contributes to your programming. Someone educated (programmed) in the memes of French will behave differently in France from someone who has no knowledge of the language—his mind will recognize meaning where others will hear only noise. Someone programmed with the distinction Coca-Cola will be more likely to buy Coke than the store brand of cola. Her mind will recognize the familiar red can with the white swish; the store brand will not register because she has no distinction-meme for it.

The Coca-Cola Company knows this, by the way, which is why their logo has grown bigger and bigger over the years until today the entire front panel of a six-foot-tall Coke machine bears the distinctive red and white trademark.

Advertisers, politicians, and anyone else who wants your money or support are very interested in programming you with certain distinctions over others and understanding the distinctions you see the world through so that they can take advantage of them. What are you more likely to buy for breakfast: a slice of chocolate cake or a "chocolate-chip muffin"? Calling a round piece of high-fat chocolate cake a "muffin" takes advantage of the distinctions you have around breakfast food and increases sales. My local café has just come out with scone-shaped brownies! Of course, not many people would eat brownies for breakfast, but scones . . . ?!

Strategy-memes

Another kind of meme is a *strategy,* a kind of floating rule of thumb that tells you what to do when you come across an applicable situation in order to achieve some desired result. For example, if you drive, you have a set of distinction-memes having to do with driving: traffic lights, speed limits, lane markers, and so on. You also have a set of strategy-memes giving you your driving behavior:

- When you come to a red light and you want to turn right, stop and then turn.

- At a four-way stop, wait for all the cars that were there ahead of you to go, then *you* go.

- When you get to a traffic circle, go counterclockwise.

- When you see a cop, slow down.

The effect of all these strategy-memes is that you avoid accidents, get where you're going, or avoid being ticketed. You can see these strategy-memes at work unconsciously every day. It's not unusual to see people who are not speeding step on the brake when they pass a police car. Traffic circles in foreign countries are particularly difficult for people used to driving on the other side of the road because they have to consciously override several learned strategies. And if you've ever seen four drivers come to a four-way stop simultaneously, you have an idea how behavior becomes unpredictable when people's strategy-memes suddenly don't apply.

Since the future is unpredictable, strategy-memes are never cast-in-stone Truths about how to behave. All strategy-memes are approximations, based on the idea that if you behave in a certain way, you'll have a certain effect on the world.

> Strategies are beliefs about cause and effect. When you are programmed with a strategy-meme, you unconsciously believe behaving a certain way is likely to produce a certain effect. That behavior may trigger a chain of events that results in spreading the strategy-meme to another mind.

As the world changes and as you change and grow, the relationship between cause and effect changes, too. For instance, people learn many of their strategies for relating to people by the time they are five years old. Often those aren't the most powerful strategies to use as adults.

For example, a two-year-old boy might become programmed with a strategy-meme for sulking. He might copy this behavior from another child or learn, through trial and error, that sulking brings extra attention and love. Either way, he now has this strategy-meme as part of his mental programming, waiting for an applicable situation to fire up and take effect. His mother is on the phone? Sulk. She ends the call and comes over to give the kid some attention. Other people's mothers may respond better to tantrums, cajoling, or smiles—their kids would get programmed with appropriate strategy-memes to that environment. In other words, your parents' behavior directs a lot of your initial programming.

Thirty years later, that two-year-old boy is now a 32-year-old man in a job where he doesn't feel appreciated. He may still be programmed with that strategy-meme he acquired at the age of two. However, sulking in that new scenario probably wouldn't cause as satisfying a result as it did when he was a child. Unfortunately, he doesn't even realize he's doing it.

As adults, we have the power and tools to influence others far beyond what we had as two-year-olds. The problem is that our heads are full of old strategy-memes, and we have office buildings full of adults sulking, throwing tantrums, cajoling, and smiling in an unconscious and ineffective effort to satisfy some unmet need.

> We often don't realize we're programmed with strategy-memes, and the ones we have are often ineffective. Understanding the strategy-memes we're programmed with gives us the power to consciously choose which strategies to follow using our full brainpower.

Association-memes

A third kind of meme is an *association,* which links two or more memes in your mind. For instance, if I smell creosote—and I only know it's creosote because I have a distinction-meme for creosote—I associate it with the Boston waterfront from my childhood, where my dad would take me on special occasions. I like that smell. It reminds me of happy times. If advertisers knew I liked it and if other people liked it just as much, we'd soon see creosote-smelling ads for vacation spots to take advantage of that association.

Said in another way, I have a certain *attitude* about creosote. I have attitudes about my work, about all the people in my life, about television, about memes—about everything. These attitudes are memes that associate other memes with one another so that when we are present to one, we become present to the other.

Advertisers don't wait for you to develop your own association-memes. They go ahead and program you with theirs through television:

- Baseball, hot dogs, apple pie, and Chevrolet

- Sexy men and Diet Coke

- Sexy women and beer

- Sexy women and computers, cars, garden tools,
  fan belts . . .

Being programmed with association-memes influences your behavior. This is the classic experiment Pavlov performed on his dog: He rang a bell each time he was about to feed it. Soon the dog developed an association-meme: the bell and food. When the programming was complete, the dog began to salivate upon hearing the bell. Advertisers want you to salivate, or the sexual equivalent, when you see their product.

There's a potential quibble here over whether all such associations—or all strategies, for that matter—are memes, or whether some are just plain old behavioral programming, which we know all about and wouldn't require a beautiful new theory such as memetics to explain. Well, the world is very complex. If being programmed with an association causes any change in your behavior, then it makes sense to consider that bit of programming a potential meme, looking to see if there's any possibility that the change in your behavior will end up creating copies of the association in others. If you go to a baseball game and say, "Did you know Ken Griffey, Jr., drives a Chevy?" you've just passed on your association-meme to someone else.

> Associations are connections between memes. When you are programmed with an association-meme, the presence of one thing triggers a thought or feeling about something else. This causes a change in your behavior, which can ultimately spread the meme to another mind.

Association-memes are subtle, and their exploitation can be insidious. Cults program their members with association-memes linking good feelings with the teachings of the group. It takes only a short time for people to believe that their quality of life, or perhaps their very survival, depends on staying in the cult—that they should be grateful for the cult giving them life.

In Chapter 8, we'll see how those of us who are not cult members may have the same kind of programming—if not quite so intense—about the company we work for, capitalism, democracy, our family, our religion, and our spouse.

The Effect of Programming

As any copyright lawyer can tell you, people don't own ideas. You can copyright the *expression* of an idea, artistic or otherwise: you can own the rights to a painting, novel, poem, or symphony based on whatever ideas you want; but you can't own an idea. In fact, the reverse is often true: ideas sometimes own people. And ideas are made up of memes.

> Memes can and do run your life, probably to a far greater degree than you realize.

How can a meme own you? The most straightforward way is through the laws and customs of your society. Men's and women's roles in society, for instance, were ruled a hundred years ago by memes that seem odd, offensive, or even ridiculous today: *A woman's place is in the home; Behind every great man there is a woman; A woman ought not make waves;* and so on. Out of these memes came a loss of opportunity for both women and men.

That changed only when a few committed people refused to buy into those memes and worked to pry them out of people's minds and replace them with new ones: *equal opportunity; A woman can be anything she wants to be; A woman without a man is like a fish without a bicycle;* and so on. Those old sexist memes severely limited women's options in life just because most people were programmed with them.

The laws we live under are another example of how memes rule us. While not many would argue with laws against crimes such as murder, other laws seem a bit more arbitrary, yet greatly affect the way people live their lives. In the former Soviet Union, people lived under laws that forbade speaking out against the government and criminalized making a profit; while in the United States, people go to prison for growing marijuana and "insider trading," violating the rules of the stock market.

The price of civilization is compromise. Without general agreement on millions of ideas, big and small, the incredibly complex society we have built would quickly disintegrate.

> Just think what life would be like if most of us did not agree on the memes of property ownership, contracts, what the colors on traffic lights mean, or saving and withdrawing money from a bank.

Take a look at just the distinction-meme of money! What if one day we all changed our minds about the idea of what money was used for and what it was worth and discovered a bunch of dirty green pieces of paper in our pockets? Something like this happened, by the way, in post–World War II Eastern Europe in times of hyperinflation.

These broad, societal memes are too many to enumerate, yet they have tremendous influence over the way we live our lives. Not all of them have such a good/bad flavor to them, as do our sex roles, yet we need to understand that they are all artificial, man-made, and in most cases not a proud result of conscious choice such as the U.S. Constitution. Most of these memes, like the pre-20th-century sex roles, just sort of evolved without anybody seriously questioning them. It is, of course, nothing new to question societal norms. People throughout history have written about the silliness of living in a cage of arbitrary social rules. But the task of changing those rules is difficult.

> It *is possible* to shift the dominant memes that constitute a society, but because of the way viruses of the mind spread ideas, it's not a straightforward task to do so.

Memetics gives those who understand it the opportunity to better influence the spread of memes.

Peer Pressure

Slavery to memes doesn't stop at the national level. Any group of people who interact with each other is subject to *peer pressure:* the pressure on each individual to behave and think as the rest of the group does. Peer pressure often gets the blame for inducing children to smoke, take drugs, and join gangs; but adults are also subject to it.

Recovering alcoholics sometimes make the decision to give up their friends who drink in order to escape the crushing peer pressure, and they join Alcoholics Anonymous to intentionally subject themselves to more constructive peer pressure. Companies such as Microsoft, where I worked for many years, have an elaborate internal culture that constantly reinforces certain memes; in Microsoft's case, elitism, commitment, intolerance of shoddiness, and hard work were large parts of that culture.

When people get immersed in a culture with strong new memes, it tends to be a sink-or-swim proposition. Either you change your mind, succumbing to peer pressure and adopting the new memes as your own, or you struggle with the extremely uncomfortable feeling of being surrounded by people who think you're crazy or inadequate. The fact that you probably think the same thing about them is little consolation.

Other subcultures have different ethics from Microsoft, but the results are the same. For instance, many of my friends who have worked in government tell me of a culture almost opposite to that of Microsoft: indifference, tolerance of shoddiness ("close enough for government work"), punching out at 5, and mediocrity as expressed by the ubiquitous sign "It's tough to soar with the eagles when you have to work with the turkeys." Immersion in that culture has the same effect: either you adopt those memes or you struggle against the peer pressure.

Your Personal Programming

The memes you are personally programmed with, even without considering the culture around you, affect your life in almost every conceivable way. That's why a virus of the mind is something to be taken seriously. These viruses fill your mind up with memes—ideas, attitudes, and beliefs—that make the results you get in life very different from the results you may want.

> One of the ways the memes you are programmed with greatly affect your future is through *self-fulfilling prophecy.*

Believing that something will happen often makes it more *likely* to happen. A child who is told repeatedly by parents that she is a successful person who can be anything she wants to be is programmed for success (at least by her parents' standards); while a child who grows up parentless in the inner city, seeing nothing but failure and despair, is likewise programmed for failure. Mind viruses often fill our heads with self-sabotaging attitudes—memes—that hinder us from making the most of our lives.

Self-fulfilling prophecy is the reason psychics and horoscopes can work. There's an excellent psychic named Maxwell who works in a local Seattle restaurant. I say "excellent" because I've seen him work twice. Both times he gave tarot-card readings to friends of mine that predicted health, wealth, and happiness, provided they seized the opportunity to pursue their life passion and acted soon.

Being a bit of an amateur prestidigitator, I noticed how he rigged the cards so that the right three would come up in what's known in the magic biz as a "force"—the client believes he has chosen the cards of his own free will. The card trick added to Maxwell's credibility and made it more likely that people would take his advice. I hope they did—it's a great self-fulfilling prophecy likely to program anyone for a rich, full life!

Aside from steering our futures, the distinction-memes we're programmed with form a *perceptual filter* on the immediate-present world around us. People cannot take in any more than a small fraction of all the information that hits their sensory organs every second. What information do we take in, and what do we filter out? Our unconscious minds decide for us, based on the distinction-memes we are programmed with.

> The distinction-memes you are programmed with control what information you perceive. They actually make reality look different to you.

Most people haven't consciously trained their minds to look for the information that is most important to them—quite a difficult and lengthy process, one I touch on in Chapter 12—so that choice is left up to chance and the influence of mind viruses.

Examples of perceptual filters abound: Ever buy a new car and suddenly notice dozens of others like it on the road where you hadn't before? You've got a new distinction-meme. If a friend notices the new car you bought out of your new distinction-meme and starts seeing them all over the road, you've just spread that meme to another mind.

Ever learn a new word and suddenly see it everywhere? That word was there all the time: you just didn't notice it because you didn't have a distinction-meme for it. If you start using it, or tell a friend how odd it is that you've been seeing this word all over the place, you've just spread the meme to another mind.

I have a friend who used to enjoy listening to Pachelbel's Canon in D Major until I pointed out to him that it sounded a lot like the old Burger King jingle; now every time he hears it, all he can think about is "Hold the pickle, hold the lettuce. . . ." Being programmed with the distinction-meme *Burger King jingle,* he has no choice but to recognize that melody whenever he hears his former favorite piece. He hates me.

Advertising works by altering your perceptual filter to pay more attention to, or have better feelings toward, the advertiser's product. Politicians with their slogans and rhetoric hope to infect your mind with memes that make you perceive them as a good choice to vote for.

The world is full of memes spread by mind viruses, all competing for a share of your mind, your perception, your attention. They care nothing for your well-being, but instead add to your confusion and subtract from your fulfillment.

Your attitudes about the past also influence your life. A current trend in America is to label more and more people "victims" of cruel, unfair, or neglectful treatment in their pasts. While it's certainly a valid point of view, those who look upon themselves as victims of their personal histories typically experience continuing emotional pain and a feeling of powerlessness.

A good course in self-empowerment trains people to view themselves as accountable for their entire lives, even those unfair and victimizing events of the past. Once people make this sometimes difficult shift in attitude—in their memetic programming—they often go through a relatively brief period of grief or sadness, followed by an experience of letting go and moving forward with their lives.

The Truth Trap

What did Alfred North Whitehead mean, in the quote that begins Chapter 1, that there are no whole truths, only half-truths? I used that quote because the distinction-meme *Truth,* meaning absolute fact or authority, is not part of the new paradigm of memetics.

The truth of any proposition depends upon the assumptions you make in considering it—the distinction-memes you use in thinking about it. You might say that the sun rises in the east and sets in the west. Is that true? Maybe it's more accurate to say that the earth orbits the sun. But is *that* true? Really, everything in the universe is influenced to a small degree by everything else. But if you're building a ballpark and you want to put home plate where the sun won't get in the batters' eyes, saying the sun sets in the west is a great meme to use—a useful half-truth. If you're in charge of building the ballpark and you start talking to the construction workers about relativity and gravitational theory, you're unlikely to get the results you want.*

What about all those eternal questions whose answers might be called eternal truths? Is there life after death? Depends on what you mean by *life,* by *death* . . . even by *is!* It's dangerous to latch onto one answer without remembering the assumptions present in the question. Every time you have a new set of distinction-memes, you have a whole new philosophy.

Labeling a meme *True* lodges it in your programming and eliminates your conscious ability to choose your own memes. Once some authority convinces you something is True or Right or is something you Should do, you are effectively programmed. If you realize there are only half-truths—that the truth of any meme depends on the context in which it exists—you have a powerful weapon against the programming of mind viruses.

Do you obey rules or any form of authority other than yourself? Laws, your superiors at work, doctors, parents . . . ? I hope you are respectful of your fellow inhabitants of the planet, but I also hope you realize that anytime you're obeying instructions, you're ripe for exploitation by mind viruses. As you'll see in Chapter 3, viruses work by taking instruction-obeying mechanisms and

---

*Even the half-truth "The sun sets in the west" has questionable assumptions. I was standing on my deck in Seattle on the Fourth of July watching a beautiful sunset when it occurred to me: *Hey! The sun's setting in the north!* Sure enough, from my west-facing deck, I had to turn a full 90 degrees to see the sun set.

What was going on? First, it wasn't True that my deck faced west. In Seattle, we tend to call the direction that faces Puget Sound's Elliott Bay "west"; however, where I live there's a bend in the shoreline so that the water-facing direction is actually more southwest.

Second, the sun really doesn't always set in the west! North of the Arctic Circle, of course, there are summer days when the sun doesn't set at all; it just kind of dips toward the North Pole, then starts back up again. If you're right below the Arctic Circle—say, in Finland—you have one really short night at the summer solstice where the sun just barely flits below the horizon—*directly north!* Down in Seattle, during the long days and short nights surrounding the summer solstice, the sun sets and rises pretty far north. Those two half-truths combined to give me my "northern sunset." (Thanks to William Calvin for this commonsense "proof" of northern sunsets.)

co-opting them. If you are an instruction-obeying mechanism, you will be co-opted, no doubt about it.

What can we do about it? For most of us, it doesn't work to shut ourselves out of all cultural institutions. Participating in jobs, relationships, clubs, and judicial systems seems essential or at least practical in our attempts to make lives for ourselves. But to avoid becoming enslaved by mind viruses, we need to pick and choose. "Question Authority" is probably the best bumper-sticker advice ever given, so long as you don't read it to mean "Contradict Authority": mind viruses have just as big a field day with automatic rebels as with automatic yes-men.

> Both rebels and yes-men behave predictably according to their memetic programming.

The point is to understand that you *have* memetic programming so you can reprogram yourself when mind-virus infections are interfering with your life!

A mind virus thrives on your belief that its memes are True. People defend the memes they're programmed with like they were protecting their own lives! It's the mind virus's paradise: it has co-opted your intelligence and problem-solving ability in order to preserve itself.

The only way we learn and grow is by changing our belief systems—changing our memetic programming. Yet, paradoxically, we tend to hang on to that programming as if it would kill us to be wrong about any of our memes.

Cultural institutions—countries, businesses, organizations—are nothing more than the results of cultural evolution, exploiting whatever resources were available as they evolved. There is nothing sacred about any of them unless you choose to make it so. Wherever there are masses of people confused about their own purpose in life and willing to take orders, cultural institutions will spring up to exploit them. Rarely is such an institution consciously chosen by its populace to enhance the lives of the participants; institutions that program people with self-serving memes are the ones that win.

A cultural institution that programs people with self-serving memes is a virus of the mind. That doesn't necessarily mean it's a bad thing, but if I were you, I'd want to know which mind viruses were competing for use of my life so that I could at least pick and choose among them, if not invent my own.

According to the new paradigm of memetics, the mind works as a combination of instinct and memetic programming. It's possible to consciously choose your own memetic programming to better serve whatever purpose you choose, upon reflection, to have for your life. Without understanding memetics, though, the programming people have tends to be whatever they happened to get as they went through childhood and life. As you'll see in the next few chapters, much of that programming is the result of infection by mind viruses. To begin to see that, take a look at what a virus is and how it works.

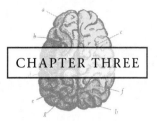

CHAPTER THREE

VIRUSES

*"Imagine that there is a nickelodeon in the
local bar which, if you press buttons 11-U,
will play a song whose lyrics go this way:*

*Put another nickel in, in the nickelodeon,
All I want is 11-U, and music, music, music."*

— Douglas Hofstadter, *Gödel, Escher, Bach*

Long ago, possibly billions of years ago, there arose through evolution a new type of organism—if it can even be called an organism. The new thing had the unusual property that it could invade the reproductive facilities of other organisms and put them to use making copies of itself. We call this creature a *virus*.

Viruses exist in three universes that we know of:

— The first is the universe of **biology**, of organisms . . . of people, plants, and animals. It's where viruses were first discovered: tobacco plants get them, and so do we. There are countless varieties of biological viruses on Earth and countless copies of each. They remain the cause of some of our most deadly and least curable or understood diseases, ranging from the common cold to AIDS or worse.

— The second universe where viruses exist is the man-made world of **computers**, networks, data, and programming. Viruses weren't discovered in this world; rather, they were invented— programmed.

In one of the best-known incidents of inventing a computer virus, Robert Morris, Jr., a student at Cornell University, tried an unauthorized experiment on a government-funded nation-wide computer network in November 1988. He wrote a program designed to make copies of itself and install one on each computer in the network.

A small error in the program, however, caused it to keep going after it was supposed to stop, clogging up the entire network with millions of copies of itself and crippling the network for hours. Government officials considered this bit of hacking so serious that they charged the astonished student with federal crimes. His program, which became known as the *Internet worm,* was a form of computer virus. He had tapped into the almost limitless power a virus has once unleashed, and at the same time experienced the loss of any control over the virus by its creator.

By now the term *computer virus* is well known. But this electronic form of virus proves to be almost as difficult to cure as the biological kind. An antivirus industry has sprung up around it, capitalizing on the fact that computer programs are much easier to understand than DNA. Regular updates of programs with names like Vaccine, Dr. Virus, and AntiVirus keep computers free of all the known strains, but vandals continue to create more and more. The high speed, excellent communication, and large storage capabilities of computers make them an attractive target for delinquents and a welcoming environment for viruses.

— The third universe is the main subject of this book: the universe of the **mind**, of culture, of thought. This is the universe in which the paradigm shift is taking place. From an old model of cultural evolution based on innovation and conquest, we are shifting to a new model based on memetics and viruses of the mind. Mind viruses are both discovered and invented: they can evolve naturally or be created consciously.

Biology	Computers	Mind
gene	machine instruction	meme
cell	computer	mind
DNA	machine language	internal brain representation of knowledge
virus	computer virus	virus of the mind
gene pool	all software	meme pool
spores/germs	electronic bulletin-board postings	broadcasts/publications
species	operating system	cultural institution
genus & higher classifications	machine architecture program	culture
organism	"back door" or security hole	behavior/artifact
genetic susceptibility	artificial life	psychological susceptibility or "button"
genetic evolution		cultural evolution

Viruses occur in three different universes: biology, computers, and the mind. This table shows the correspondence between words used to talk about evolution and viruses in each of the three universes.

In 1978, in a small village in Guyana, a closely knit community of people purposely killed themselves by drinking a mixture of cyanide, Valium, and Fla-Vor-Aid. They knew they would die. As to what else they knew, we can only speculate. Did they "know" that a far greater reward awaited them in the next life? Did they "know" that obeying the orders of Jim Jones, their leader, was their duty? Did they "know" that if they just followed their faith, everything would turn out all right? It's pretty clear what they "knew" hurt them: they didn't drink that poison out of instinct—they were following the programming of some memes that resulted in their deaths.

Why has Pepsi spent millions of dollars broadcasting commercials that show people drinking their product while endlessly repeating "Uh-huh"? Why do some outlandish stories get endlessly perpetuated as "urban legends"? Why do some chain letters travel around and around the world, seemingly unstoppable?

The answers to those questions all have to do with viruses of the mind. The mind has all the properties a virus needs to exist, just as do cells and computers. In fact, our society of instant communication and access to information is improving daily as a gracious host to mind viruses.

What Is a Virus?

Keeping in mind that the virus concept applies to all three realms—biology, computer, and mind—let's start by looking at the workings of biological viruses.

We can't talk about viruses without talking about copying. That's what a virus does, after all: it makes copies of itself. That wouldn't be of much more than intellectual interest to us if it were not for one fact: a virus uses *us* as its laboratory for making copies of itself, frequently leaving a mess behind.

A virus is more than a parasite, more than an infiltrator, more than an unchecked self-copier. A virus is all of these at the same time.

> A *virus* is anything that takes external copying equipment and puts it to work making copies of itself.

One reason to take viruses seriously is that making copies of yourself—self-replicating—is the most powerful force in the universe.* Where there was once 1, now there are 2, 4, 8, 16, 32, 64, 128, 256, 512. . . . Growth by doubling is called *exponential growth,* and it works very quickly to fill up whatever space is available. An atomic bomb works that way: One fissioned atom causes others to split, which in turn cause more atoms to split, all releasing energy. When the space available inside the bomb is filled—*kablooey!*

In the case of a typical biological virus, the copying equipment it commandeers is in the cells of the organism being attacked. Cells use that equipment in the normal course of their affairs to manufacture proteins, duplicate nucleic acids, and prepare to divide in two. The virus infiltrates the cell and fools the copying equipment into copying the virus in addition to, or instead of, its usual workload. I always conjure up a mental picture of a syringe-like virus poking its needle into a cell and injecting its own genetic program so the cell machinery starts going to work producing more syringes. There's some artistic license with this mental picture, but it helps me get the idea.

Anywhere there is copying machinery, there can be viruses. Modern computer networks, designed specifically to copy and transmit data, were a natural target for malicious or mischievous hackers to create man-made viruses, which they in fact did relatively quickly. Unlike their biological counterparts, all known computer viruses are man-made, which is to be expected since computers are designed especially to minimize *mutations,* or corruption of data.

> A *mutation* is an error in copying. It produces a defective— or possibly improved in some sense—copy instead of an exact duplicate of the original.

Since humans designed computers with the express intention of making them easy for us to program, it's not too surprising that

---

*If you had the thought that perhaps God is the most powerful force in the universe—remember: He created us in His own image. Self-replication!

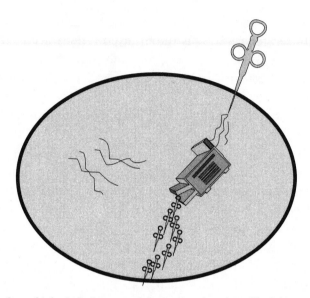

Some biological viruses work by penetrating the cell's defenses as a syringe needle penetrates skin. They inject instructions into the cell so that its duplicating machinery manufactures more syringe-like viruses. Eventually the cell bursts, and the new virus copies spread to other cells.

we've found it easy to create viruses that exist in that medium— far easier, for example, than we've found it to engineer any kind of DNA-based organism. But DNA wasn't designed by humans for the purpose of programming: it doesn't have a rational instruction set, multipurpose registers, or internationally approved input/output interface standards. My guess is that it will be a long time before we learn to create an organism from scratch out of DNA the way computer programmers create software from scratch out of programming languages.*

A virus can exist anywhere there is copying going on. For billions of years, the only significant copying going on was that

---

*When it does happen, though, it will probably be through the use of higher-level languages that "compile" a genetic engineer's intentions into DNA strands the way the C computer-programming language compiles a computer programmer's intentions into *machine language,* the actual instructions the computer executes. When we figure that out, that's when we'll start seeing Walmart sell living "vacuum cleaners" that scurry about our houses at night eating dirt off the floors and carpets. And the possibilities for the adult-entertainment industry are endless, if morally disturbing.

of DNA and associated molecules. We've learned a lot about the physical mechanism by which DNA gets copied, but it's still quite a leap to understand how the *information* in the DNA causes a human being to self-assemble from a single cell to an adult. It's the difference between understanding how the *Encyclopedia Britannica* is printed and understanding the complete functioning of the world described in its volumes.

A virus doesn't change the way in which DNA gets copied; a virus inserts new information to be copied along with, or instead of, the rest. What happens, then, to the cell containing that new information? There are three possibilities:

1. The information may be unintelligible to the rest of the cell and have minimal effect on its workings other than perhaps to decrease its efficiency at all the other work it has to do.

2. The information may confuse or sabotage the workings of the cell and cause it to malfunction, at least from some point of view. (From the virus's point of view, the new functioning may be fine.)

3. The information may improve the cell's functioning by giving it some kind of new ability or defense mechanism.

Just Obeying Orders

A virus takes advantage of the fact that the copying mechanism doesn't have a good screening system to ensure that it is only copying approved data. In the case of a cell, the copying mechanism copies instructions to the cell's inner workings about which proteins to manufacture. Those proteins, in turn, control the various chemical reactions that chart the course of a cell's life: a time to store sugars, a time to manufacture oxygen, a time to split, a time to die. The virus's sneaky tactics are like the insane officer's orders to the bomber squadron in *Dr. Strangelove* to launch an unprovoked attack on Moscow: the cell, or bomber crew, just obeys its new instructions and off it goes.

One of the instructions that the virus gives is to manufacture more viruses and in some way spread them to other hosts. This particular instruction is essential or the virus would quickly die out. The spreading can be direct, as a cell that fills so full of viruses that it bursts; or indirect, as a virus that induces sneezing and a virus-rich runny nose.

Computer viruses work the same way. First the vandal programmer inserts the virus code into some other program that she expects will be run by unsuspecting users. When it *is* run, the virus code quickly copies itself into some or all of the other programs it detects on the computer. As soon as one of those infected programs gets copied, by humans or automatically, onto another computer and is run, the new computer becomes infected and the process begins anew.

Putting aside the social implications of this form of vandalism, let's look at the common elements between biological and computer viruses:

- Something foreign gets inserted into an environment.

- Copying takes place in that environment.

- There is some kind of instruction-following going on in that environment.

- The foreign body gets copied, possibly issues new instructions, and spreads to new environments so the process can continue.

What Makes a Good Virus?

A successful virus must let its host live long enough to spread the virus. That's odd, though—wouldn't it follow that the most successful viruses would let the host keep living and spreading them as long as possible? Wouldn't that mean we should expect viruses to be on our side in general, since our health is linked to their survival?

That depends on what you mean by "on our side." The success of a virus in the long run depends on its ability to replicate without killing its hosts. Of course, that doesn't help you if you're killed by one that hasn't evolved to be "successful" yet. As John Maynard Keynes pointed out, in the long run we're all dead. A virus that spread to ten other people and killed you in the process would be quite successful enough, short term. A virus that immediately killed *every* host wouldn't be successful, just as a computer virus that instantly crashed every computer it infected wouldn't last long. But longevity of the host is just one possibility for a virus's mission:

> A virus's mission is to make as many copies of itself as possible.

Wait a minute—why is that the virus's mission? Do we really believe that viruses have some kind of guiding purpose to their lives? What does it even mean to say that a virus has a mission? Why couldn't a virus just be content with infecting one cell, retiring, and kicking back and watching the endoplasmic reticulum for the rest of its days?

The short answer is: if it did, it wouldn't be a virus as it's defined here. I'm only using the word *virus* to refer to things that penetrate, copy, possibly issue instructions, and spread. But waving my hands and clinging to the definition is the easy way out. There's a very subtle point here, one that's important to understand because it runs through this entire book:

> When we look at life from the point of view of a virus, we're *not* saying the virus is alive, can think, or even *has* a point of view.*

Looking at things from the point of view of a virus just gives us insight into what's interesting about viruses: how and why they spread.

When I say a virus's mission in life is to spread, I mean only that when we examine viruses, the interesting thing about them is that they spread. If they didn't spread, we wouldn't call them viruses and we wouldn't be interested in them. We *are* interested in viruses because their penetrating, copying, issuing of instructions, and especially spreading is a powerful force in our universe. It's fascinating, exciting, and even scary to discover something that, once released, goes off on its own and spreads itself to the world with no further effort on the part of its creator.

Saying a virus has a mission in life is a trick to make it easy to understand how it works. It would be equally correct to reverse points of view:

> The universe contains many mechanisms for copying and dispersing information, and viruses are some of the things that are often copied and dispersed.

Some of these copying mechanisms are straightforward; others are roundabout. But the viruses we see the most copies of are the ones that those mechanisms happen to latch onto and copy.

So given that we're only studying successful viruses, the one thing we know about them is that they are good at spreading. The DNA viruses have found effective ways to spread via the copying mechanisms of our cells. The criminals who create computer viruses have found effective ways to spread them via the copying

---

*This viral viewpoint is what evolutionary biologists call the *teleological fallacy:* the tendency to attribute complex evolutionary motives to dumb animals or biomolecules. What we're seeing is "knowledge" hardwired into these creatures through billions of years of evolution, not memetic thoughts like we have.

mechanisms of computers. All of which brings us to the most interesting copying mechanism of all: the human mind.

The Mind

Our minds excel both at copying information and at following instructions. Remember the four characteristics of a virus: penetration, copying, possibly issuing instructions, and spreading. As horrifying as the thought may be initially, our minds are ideally susceptible to infection by mind viruses. They can *penetrate* our minds because we are so adept at learning new ideas and information. They are *copied* by us communicating with each other, something we are getting better and better at. Mind viruses *issue instructions* by programming us with new memes that affect our behavior. They *spread* when the chain of events stemming from that new behavior reaches an uninfected mind.

Examples of viruses of the mind range from fashion fads to religious cults. They can be any bit of culture whose existence touches people, causing them to shift their thinking and thus their behavior, eventually causing reinforcement or proliferation of that same bit of culture. Chapters 9, 10, and 11 are full of examples of viruses of the mind.

At this point I want to introduce a distinction between mind viruses that arose spontaneously and ones that were invented by human consciousness. I'll call the naturally arising ones *cultural viruses* and the human-crafted ones *designer viruses*. A designer virus is carefully crafted to infect people with a set of memes that influence them to spread the virus throughout the population.

Designer viruses and cultural viruses can be equally damaging to your pursuit of happiness, although for many people it doesn't feel as bad to have your life ruined by a natural set of circumstances as it does to have some manipulative no-goodnik get the best of you. But despite the difference in perception, the effect of these two kinds of mind viruses is the same: you unwittingly have a portion of yourself diverted from what you might otherwise be doing with your life, and instead devoted to doing the work of the mind virus.

Memetics provides new insight into the way our minds, societies, and cultures work. Rather than looking at the development of culture as a sequence of ideas and discoveries that build upon one another, what would it be like to view culture as a meme pool, where the ideas in our heads are shaped and transported by various forces, including mind viruses? How many of these viruses are already with us? Are they helping or harming us? Can we control them? Can our enemies create new ones and infect us with them?

The outer reaches of this line of thought are dark and scary. However, I see much, much more potential for help than harm through understanding the mind virus. And even though it involves thinking about things in unfamiliar ways, I suggest we do whatever it takes to understand it, tame it, and put it to work for our best interests and the best interests of our children—and our children's children.

To begin that, let's take a look at one of the most misunderstood of all scientific theories: evolution by natural selection.

CHAPTER FOUR

EVOLUTION

"It is almost as if the human brain
were specifically designed to misunderstand
Darwinism, and to find it hard to believe."

— Richard Dawkins

There is no scientific theory that is both so well known and so disputed as the theory of evolution. Perhaps I should say "theories" of evolution, because even among respected scientists there is significant disagreement over just how evolution works. Outside of science, of course, we find even more disagreement, from religious fundamentalists whose faith conflicts with the evolutionary model, to New Age interpretations of evolution as a purposeful striving toward spiritual perfection, to people who just have a gut sense that evolution is too far-fetched to explain the lush variety of life on this planet.

The reason for all the disagreement, I believe, is a cloudy understanding of just what is involved in evolution. Our gut sense isn't designed to understand what happens over millions or billions of years, so it's natural to be skeptical of something that only operates over that long a period. Our fundamentalist religions operate out of faith in a certain belief system, and until now evolution was presented in a way that was difficult to reconcile with those beliefs. Our scientists spend their lives developing and discussing complex models of the way things work and naturally resist anything that doesn't fit into those models. Understanding evolution requires some fresh thinking.

Evolution and Entropy

In the broadest sense, evolution simply means that things change over time. As things change, the things that are good at sticking around and replicating themselves do so, while the other things don't.

The things that are good at sticking around and self-replicating are called *replicators.* The two most interesting replicators in the universe today—interesting both because they involve *us* and because they are evolving the fastest—are the gene, which is the basic replicator in the universe of biology, and the meme, which is the basic replicator in the universe of the mind. In the world of computers, you could look at machine instructions or programs as replicators, but at this point software is more a product of intentional crafting by human minds than of evolution by natural selection. Until we start letting software loose to evolve on its own, it's just another type of meme.*

When we use the word *evolution,* as in "the evolution of species by natural selection," we're making a distinction between the winners of that battle, which continue to exist, and the losers,

---

*Experiments in modeling evolution through computers are part of the fascinating new field known as *artificial life.* Read Steven Levy's excellent book *Artificial Life* (Vintage Books, 1993) to learn more about it.

which don't. *Natural selection* means that the forces of nature are doing the selecting, as opposed to the *artificial selection* of breeding pedigreed dogs, for example, in which people do the selecting. The things that are not good at sticking around eventually disappear through *entropy,* the tendency of things to randomize and level out over time, like sand castles on a beach or a decaying log.

> Evolution is a scientific model of how things become more complex; entropy describes how things become simpler. They are the creative and the destructive forces of the universe.

The two forces operate not only in the physical universe, but also in the realm of the mind. For example, as the English language changes through time, certain new words and usages *evolve* to encompass new distinctions that have become widespread. Through *entropy,* less-used words often lose distinctions such as subtleties of meaning or irregular spelling or pronunciation.

Making Copies

The study of evolution is the study of making copies. A replicator is anything that gets copied. Sometimes a replicator seems to do more than just "get copied" passively; it seems to take a more active role. Perhaps it could be said to "make copies of itself." The difference is merely a matter of point of view. Sometimes it will seem more natural to think of a replicator as making copies of itself, as when cells split and DNA duplicates. At other times, it will make more sense to think of a replicator as something that just happens to get copied, as when people hum a catchy tune or the idea of democracy spreads throughout the world. In all cases, the copying happens, which is what evolution needs.

> Anything at all that gets copied—no matter what the copying mechanism, and whether or not there is a conscious intention to copy—is a *replicator.*

Sometimes mistakes get made in copying. That's necessary for evolution to take place. If the fidelity of the copies is too high, nothing ever changes. If it's too low, you don't really have a replicator: soon the quality that made the thing good at replicating will be lost, just as a copy of a copy of a copy of an office memorandum becomes illegible.

> Evolution requires two things: replication, with a certain degree of fidelity; and innovation, or a certain degree of infidelity.

Fitness

Of course, if only one or two copies ever get made of a replicator, it's not a particularly interesting one for the purpose of understanding evolution. We're interested in replicators that produce enough high-fidelity copies of themselves that those copies in turn become replicators, and the resultant exponential growth quickly produces a large number of copies. When we talk about *survival of the fittest,* we mean survival of the thing that's best at replicating—at having copies of itself made.

> *Fitness,* in evolution, means the likelihood of being copied. The *fitter* something is, the greater its chances of being copied.

The word *fit,* in our model of how evolution works, means nothing more than that. There is no connotation of strength, agility, longevity, or extraordinary intelligence. If a replicator is fit, it is good at replicating. That's all.

It's tempting to think that a durable, long-lived replicator might compete successfully against a shorter-lived one that is better at being copied, but mathematics shows that this is not the case. Imagine two replicators: Methuselah lives 100 years and makes a copy of itself every year, for a total of 100 children; Thumper lives only one year but makes three copies of itself before it dies. This table shows how the total population of each would look after each year:

	Methuselah	Thumper
1	2	3
2	4	9
3	8	27
4	16	81
. . .	. . .	. . .
100	~10^{30}	~10^{48}

Now 10^{30}—a one with 30 zeros after it—may seem like a lot of Methuselahs. However, after 100 years, there would be approximately 10^{18} *times* more of the prolific Thumpers than the long-lived Methuselahs—that's 1,000,000,000,000,000,000 Thumpers for every Methuselah. And that's assuming the Thumpers don't start eating the Methuselahs for dinner.

The fittest replicators make the most copies of themselves and therefore become more abundant than the rest. *Survival of the fittest* is just a bit misleading; it's more like *abundance of the fittest*. Of course, if resources are scarce, the gain of the fittest replicators is at the expense of those less fit.

The Selfish Gene

All this brings us to Dawkins's *selfish gene*. The selfish-gene theory, in one flash of insight, answered so many sticky questions and puzzling details of evolution that it paralleled the astronomical discovery that the earth was not the center of the universe.

While Dawkins popularized the selfish-gene theory in the same 1976 book in which he introduced the word *meme*, credit for the first publication of the idea goes to British biologist William D. Hamilton in 1963. Prior to Hamilton's work, most scientists had assumed evolution revolved around "us," or *individuals* of whatever species we are discussing. The Darwinian idea was that evolution proceeded by the fittest individuals surviving and reproducing more individuals like themselves. Darwin's brilliant insight—the theory of evolution by natural selection—explained the facts well enough that it held on for a long time. But Darwin had never heard of DNA.

The selfish-gene theory shifted the evolutionary spotlight from the fittest individuals onto the fittest DNA. After all, it is the DNA that carries the information passed from one generation to the next. The individuals of a species don't, strictly speaking, *replicate* copies of themselves. Parents don't clone themselves to produce children who are exact copies. Instead, they cause copies of pieces of DNA to be *reproduced* in a new individual. The pieces of DNA that are best at causing themselves to get replicated become most numerous, and it is *they* that participate in "survival of the fittest," not whole individuals.

Those pieces of DNA that play this game, causing themselves to be replicated by whatever means, are called *genes*. The fact that evolution seems to revolve around their well-being rather than ours makes them *selfish genes*.

Paradoxically, one way that scientists confirm the selfish-gene theory is by noticing *unselfish* behavior in animals. Female worker bees have evolved to labor all their lives to support their mother, the queen, and have no children themselves, because by a genetic quirk their mother's offspring share more DNA with them than their own offspring would. It serves their selfish genes better to behave that way than to go off on their own.

Mothers, throughout the animal kingdom, will take great risks to save their children. Suppose a mother confronts a predator that she, but not her two children, could escape from, and there's a 50 percent chance of getting herself and her brood killed and a 50 percent chance of saving herself and her children. Since each child inherits at least half* of the mother's DNA, mathematics tells us that the DNA responsible for that tendency will have an advantage over competing DNA that would direct her to abandon the kids and save herself. Confronting the predator will, on average,

---

*Since the father shares some of the same DNA, the child may in fact have more than half.

leave more copies of the *Protect the kids* gene in the world than running away leaves of the *Save yourself* gene.

All of biological evolution has been a contest between pieces of DNA to see which genes could make the most copies of themselves.

> From a gene's point of view, a human being is just a way of making more genes.

Another Point of View

The trick to understanding genetic evolution, then, is to look at it from the point of view of the pieces of DNA competing for replication. To help do that, let's take a look at life from the point of view of some arbitrary DNA replicator. Let's call him Dan.

Now when I talk about Dan and about looking at life from Dan's point of view, I'm not implying that Dan has a consciousness, eyes, a soul, or anything like that. I'm just suggesting that we, as intelligent human beings, take a look at a model of evolution that centers around Dan, just as astronomers found that a model of our solar system that revolves around the sun was more useful than one that revolved around the earth.

Dan's situation in life is much like a university professor's: publish or perish. In Dan's case, what he's publishing are copies of everyone's favorite subject: himself. Does Dan *care* if he publishes or perishes? Only in some mystical, metaphysical sense. Dan is just a lump of carbon and a hank of amino acids. It wouldn't be fair to say he *cares* about anything. *We* may care, having grown to love and cherish him now that we've given him a name, but in reality Dan's demise would simply mean that the atoms of the universe would be arranged in a slightly different way. The DNA replication mechanism would chug away, publishing copies of Don, Diane, Denise, Doug, and Arturo. Life would go on.

But let's assume Dan is one of those DNA chunks that fares quite well at replication, so well that you can find Dan in 100 percent of the human race, not to mention quite a few chimps, baboons, and apes. In fact, you can trace Dan back to the earliest mammals, and even back to fish. Wow! Dan must be a gene for something pretty important, right? Dan must be the genetic recipe for our backbone or bloodstream or central nervous system, right? How else could Dan have survived so long, without being a gene for something extremely important to our survival?

Ah. Back up. I was looking at things from my own point of view. I can forgive myself for that, since it's human nature, but let's get back to Dan's point of view. It turns out that all Dan does is produce an enzyme that splices more copies of Dan into DNA strands. That's it. All Dan does is protect his own job. (At this point any resemblance to university professors is purely coincidental.)

Dan is not a gene "for" anything that enhances the survival of human beings. He doesn't need to be, any more than human beings need to do anything to keep the sun shining. Dan lives in a DNA factory and simply has the right stuff to replicate in that environment. As I write this, research continues to show that vast stretches of DNA in our own chromosomes seem to have no effect on our development. Surprising if we believe that evolution revolves around us, but from Dan's point of view it's no more surprising than the fact that much of what we humans do does nothing to benefit the survival of the earth.

Dan is nothing more than a piece of DNA that is good at replicating in his environment. That environment consists of:

— The cells of our body and all the mechanisms within those cells that are set up to replicate DNA.

— The other DNA that happens to reside in the same cell as Dan. Without that other DNA, some of which does cause our bodies and minds to develop and reproduce, Dan would perish with us.

— Us, living our lives and doing what we do. We don't live quite as long as elephants, which also host Dan, but we're much more prolific . . . and we're great hosts, at least until we cure cancer,

Evolution through Selfish Genes

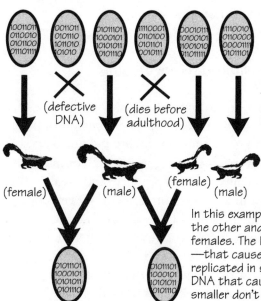

Fertilized eggs each have a unique pattern of DNA information.

Machinery in the egg cell reads the DNA code and follows its instructions, resulting (if all goes well) in an adult organism.

(defective DNA)

(dies before adulthood)

Differences in DNA affect, for example, size and coloration, resulting in better or worse success in survival and mating.

(female)   (male)   (female)   (male)

In this example, one male is bigger than the other and ends up mating with both females. The DNA codes—selfish genes —that caused him to be bigger get replicated in some of his offspring. The DNA that caused the other male to be smaller don't get replicated at all.

Genes, encoded in DNA, can be thought of as a computer program running on the "hardware" of a cell. The program "outputs" an organism, whose "mission" is to spread copies of its DNA program by mating with other such organisms.

which, by wildly replicating great quantities of Dan, was one of his little pleasures in life.

— Our environment. Dan was having great success with dinosaurs until something happened out there. Fortunately, he had hedged his bets, holding shares in some other organisms at the time, but a few of his genetic friends had too many eggs in one basket and got wiped out with the dinosaurs.

These all work together to create an environment for Dan. Really, the whole universe is Dan's environment; his fitness as a replicator is influenced in a small or large way by everything else that exists. As the poet John Donne said, no man—or Dan—is an island.

And so we bid farewell to Dan, one heck of a fit replicator. Evolution has treated him well. But before we leave the topic of genetic evolution, let's look at one question . . .

. . . *What Exactly Is Evolution Evolving <u>Toward?</u>*

Most of us who have taken high-school biology assume that evolution is guiding us—and other animals, of course—to be fitter and fitter human beings, steadily improving the quality of life on Earth and in the universe. As time goes by, we complacently assume, the fittest of us will survive; reproduce; and create a bigger, better, and stronger human race. Animals will evolve, too, and it won't be long before the Kentucky Derby is run in under a minute or our dogs get smart enough to housebreak themselves. We say to ourselves, "What a wonderful world!"

Or maybe this notion of survival of the fittest is unappealing to you. Why should evolution steer us toward greater fertility and strength? Why should we evolve to a race of oversexed and overmuscled monsters? Why shouldn't the Stephen Hawkings and Helen Kellers of the world have a chance—after all, we have the technology to overcome so many disabilities now. Perhaps evolution will favor greater and greater intellect, or even greater and greater contributions to the world!

There's no need to argue the two points, because evolution isn't favoring either one of them.

Genetic evolution favors the replication of the fittest *DNA*. And by "fittest," I mean the best at getting replicated. So as long as we're good soldiers for DNA replicators and keep multiplying and expanding, genetic evolution will favor us. But it also favors insects, which vastly outnumber us, and of course viruses, which parasitically insert themselves into whatever replication mechanism they can find, such as us, and do quite well at it. Whether we're winning, or the insects are, or the viruses are, is simply a matter of frame of reference. It's the DNA that's evolving, and we simply play a part in it.

Evolution, Not Engineering

Evolution, of genes or memes, reflects the haphazard and baroque result of an ongoing struggle, not the product of a brilliantly engineered design.

What's the difference between evolution and engineering? Engineering is the designing of a whole out of parts suited to their individual purposes. Evolution is the process of tiny incremental changes, each making some small or large improvement in the ability of the thing to survive and reproduce. A good engineer avoids the *kluge*—jargon for the use of a part not particularly suited to its purpose. But evolution favors, even cherishes, the kluge. Suddenly finding a new purpose for a part without significantly diminishing its old function is a staple of the evolutionary process.

A classic example of an evolutionary kluge is the human eye. The nerves that connect the light-sensing cells to the brain actually come out the *front* of the retina rather than the back—the "wiring" protrudes out into the eye's field of vision. It's difficult to imagine an engineer, let alone God, designing something this way. But evolution took what it had to work with and, kluge by kluge, built an eye. You can imagine a primitive creature having a light-sensing cell that evolved over millions of years into a better and better source of vision. Back when the light-sensing cell was simple, there was no advantage in having it oriented one way or the other. By the time it had developed through kluges into a complex eye, with a focusing lens, there was no way to "redesign" it so the wires would come out the back.

It's the klugy nature of evolution that makes it so difficult to decipher DNA. If DNA worked as a computer program, with its billions of "lines of code" divided neatly into functions and subroutines, we would have reverse engineered it by now. Politicians would be vying for votes based on their views on the morality of our producing genetically engineered creatures from scratch. If DNA worked like that, genetic engineers could design (and presumably patent or copyright) any animal or organism they could envision: we would create, or perhaps pass laws against creating,

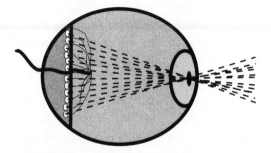

In a classic example of the klugy nature of evolution, the human eye has "wiring" that runs in front of the retina rather than behind it, as an engineer might run the wiring if designing an eye. The complexity of the eye was once thought to be evidence of a supernatural Creator, as it seemed difficult to believe that such a complex organ could evolve by natural selection. Biologists now have evidence that eyes have evolved independently, through natural selection, dozens of times in different species.

livestock that could be slaughtered for completely healthy food; special bacteria that could be injected into our bloodstream and repair cancerous tumors or eat the plaque out of arteries; even house pets that come pretrained to fetch slippers, bark at intruders, bring in the newspaper, cook dinner . . . ? Fortunately or not, the moral debate over such manufactured bio-appliances seems still quite a few years in the future.

That's because DNA and evolution do not work like a software engineer writing a computer program. DNA evolves by mutation, by little pieces of it reversing, crossing over, inserting in one place, deleting from another place, resulting in some small or large difference in the development of the embryo and finally the full-grown organism. But with minor exceptions, there is no one-to-one connection between any particular piece of DNA and a particular piece of the resultant adult organism. The DNA is not a blueprint, contrary to a popular metaphor. There is no place in the human DNA that represents the right index finger, the left little toenail.

True, scientists have found a few stretches of human DNA that, to the degree they differ between individuals, seem to map to corresponding changes in the individuals' appearance, such as eye color, blood type, or susceptibility to various diseases. But the number of these stretches is minuscule compared to the total amount of human DNA, and, as I wrote earlier, scientists seem to be coming to the conclusion that there are huge strings of genetic material in humans that appear to have no effect whatsoever on their host.

Is this surprising? Only if we look at DNA from the old animal-centric view of its function. If we look at DNA as an animal's means of reproducing itself, it makes no sense to have vast stretches of DNA that don't do anything. It's just excess baggage.

From the DNA's point of view, however, it makes perfect sense. From the point of view of genetic material, the human being that results from the presence of DNA in male and female sex cells is simply the most effective way nature has found of producing more of the same. The DNA makes use of the safety of the mother's womb to manufacture cell after cell containing copies of itself, and finally a new individual (or maybe twins) ready to go forth and help the DNA multiply yet again. We used to wonder why it was necessary for each cell to contain a complete copy of the DNA when it didn't seem to use it in any way. Well, it's not necessary; we were just being insufferably egocentric!

> From the DNA's point of view, having copies of itself is *our* whole point for existing.

There's no head-to-head competition among DNA for food or mates—we take care of all the competition *for* it—so there's little incentive for nature to remove any excess baggage from the DNA itself. It just sits in safe little nuclei, inside safe little cells, inside safe little bodies that—with the exception of human beings, who seem to have reached a new stage of evolution—devote their entire little lives to finding suitable mates that will help their host DNA replicate copies of itself.

Does that sound like an exaggeration? Not if you keep in mind that species evolved as a result of the fittest—best at replicating—DNA being selected and copied, selected and copied, over and over and over again over millions of years. Some odd characteristics and behaviors can be explained as the result of selfish-gene evolution.

The Evolution of Species

I was reading one of those collections of answers to nagging questions* such as "Why do books have blank pages at the end of them?" and "Why doesn't the 'close door' button in elevators ever do anything?" when I ran across the question "What is the purpose of the oil in the head of sperm whales?" The author quoted several authorities, each giving a credible guess at what the purpose could be. They all proposed different ways in which the oil sac might benefit the survival or reproduction of the whale, although they tended to speak as if the oil-storage mechanism were designed by an engineer rather than evolved through the natural selection of DNA.

The overall purpose of any trait developed through evolution is to make copies of some replicator—the DNA that causes that trait to develop. Usually that means the trait helps the animal do one of two things: survive or reproduce. In the case of the sperm whale's oil sac, it probably does help the whale survive, and perhaps evolved from whales without an oil sac, or with just a little oil sac, or with a sac in some other part of the body—we don't know.

But there are other possibilities. While the alliance between DNA replicators and their host animals is a strong alliance, it's not a perfect one. Sometimes the best interest of the DNA is not the best interest of the host. I'll use the sperm whale for a hypothetical example.

Suppose that years ago sperm whales had no oil sacs. Suddenly, through mutation or variation, one male whale was born with an oil sac that made his head a bit larger, but at the expense of taking up some brain space and reducing his swimming speed, both of which made him more susceptible to predators and less able to find food, and therefore lowered his life expectancy.

---

*Feldman, David. *When Did Wild Poodles Roam the Earth?* (HarperPerennial, 1992). Books have blank pages at the end of them because presses print many pages at a time on a single sheet called a *signature*. If the book doesn't come out to an even number of signatures, there are blank pages. The "close door" button on elevators is primarily for use by firefighters during emergency operation. Although it occasionally does close the door during normal operation, often it simply has no effect.

However, this oil-sac mutation had an interesting side effect. One of the features of male whales that female whales were sexually attracted to had been the male's larger head. When this oil sac showed up, even though it was a slight hindrance to that whale's survival, it attracted more than his share of female whales. Consequently, he spent his life doing lots of mating and passed the oil-sac gene on to half his children.

The same thing happened with his children, and very quickly the poor smaller-headed male whales were left to the bachelor life, while the larger-headed but stupider and slower ones got all the whale babes. In this hypothetical case, if it really happened this way, evolution favored the selfish DNA replicator that was responsible for the oil sac over the improvement of the whale species' survival ability. I have never heard anyone hypothesize anything like this about whales, and I used a completely made-up example just so as not to get into any arguments with evolutionary biologists, but scientists have seriously advanced similar theories about peacock feathers.

Why do some spiders, for example, have such elaborate rituals to determine the exact right member of the opposite sex to mate with, even though fertile offspring with no apparent reduction in fitness could be produced by a mating with any of several available varieties of spider? Again, we're looking at it from the spider's point of view, which doesn't reflect what happened in the course of evolution. Those elaborately finicky mating dances are the DNA's way of ensuring that the mate will have the same stretch of DNA that caused the dancing behavior.

The spider's dance is the genetic equivalent of Nintendo putting a special device in their game-playing machines that prevents other companies' game cartridges from working in their players. There may be many other brands of game cartridge that you as a customer might even prefer. But there's only one brand that ensures profits for Nintendo, just as there's only one species that guarantees DNA replication for the organism manufacturer—the DNA itself.

> Evolution always works for the benefit of selfish replicators. Usually, an animal's survival and reproduction contributes to the same end as the replicator's copying and spreading, but when there's a conflict, the replicator always wins.

The End of an Era

That's the story of *genetic* evolution, the success story of DNA, in which we play but a small supporting role. But don't despair: our stardom awaits! Other than our intellectual fascination with it, genetic evolution has little effect on our everyday lives. Worrying about genetic evolution is a little like worrying about being run over by a glacier: unless you're planning to stand still for the next few thousand years, it's just not going to have much impact. As far as our individual lives are concerned, genetic evolution is over and done with. With luck, neither your DNA nor mine will evolve during our lifetimes.

It's the end of the DNA era, but it's not the end of the story. For us, it's just the beginning. I mentioned before that humans seem to have reached a higher stage of evolution. When I say that, I'm not simply saying we're morally superior or God's chosen creatures or anything like that, true although it may be. What I mean is that our minds, lives, and cultures are affected by the evolution of something besides DNA. Because while genetic evolution happens so slowly that it even takes a leap of faith to believe in it, there's a new kind of evolution happening so fast that it leaves DNA in the Darwinian dust. It's the evolution of something even nearer and dearer to us than DNA.

Until a few thousand years ago, DNA was the foremost method in the known universe for storing and replicating information. That's why you can't talk about evolution without talking about DNA: evolution is about the replication of information, and almost all the information on Earth was stored in DNA.

Today we have another medium for storing information—one that replicates, mutates, and propagates far, far faster than DNA.

We have a medium so effective at evolution that new replicators can be created, tried, and spread wildly all in days or even hours, as compared to thousands of years for DNA. The new medium is so much more interesting and important than DNA to our daily lives that genetic evolution is virtually nonexistent by comparison. What is the name of this new, ripe, prolific medium for evolution?

It's called the *mind,* and the replicator that evolves in our minds is called the *meme.*

CHAPTER FIVE

THE EVOLUTION
OF MEMES

"An invasion of armies can be resisted,
but not an idea whose time has come."

— attributed to Victor Hugo

Once our brains evolved to the point where we could receive, store, modify, and communicate ideas, there suddenly appeared a new environment that had the two characteristics needed for evolution: copying and innovating. Our brains, which arose out of increasing usefulness in the process of keeping DNA hosts (that's us) alive and breeding, suddenly were thrust into the spotlight of evolution.

The brand-new innovation of the human mind was not just *another* arena for evolution besides the cell, it was a *far better* arena, simply because evolution takes place far more quickly. The biological forces that evolved our brains to the point where we had minds were now outdone a million times over by the new memetic forces evolving our thoughts, our society, and our culture. Evolution of the meme was assured.

> A meme is a replicator that uses the medium of our minds to replicate. Meme evolution happens because our minds are good at copying and innovating—ideas, behaviors, tunes, shapes, structures, and so on.

The Selfish Gene for Minds

We evolved, genetically, to the point where we had minds because of a selfish gene for minds, or for some precursor of minds that gave people with that gene a survival advantage. With that advantage, we survive and multiply, replicating the selfish gene for minds.

The DNA that causes us to have minds is, of course, not quite as fit as the DNA that makes insects small, fast, and hard-shelled. There are far more insects than people, and we're not even that good at winning battles with insects over who gets to live where. But our minds are certainly an advantage to us, and therefore to our host DNA, so here we are thinking deep thoughts and pretending we run the place. So be it.

From the DNA's point of view, of course, we're still here for one reason only: to go forth and multiply. But the DNA's only way to achieve its purpose is through the glacially slow process of genetic evolution, one step every 20 years or so, compared with the breakneck pace of meme evolution in which an idea mutates in the time it takes to read a sentence.

Because memetic evolution happens so much faster, most of what we do with our brains has little to do with genetic evolution. Being a genius—advancing the state of science or technology, creating art, writing plays—all these are klugy uses of our brain layered on top of the uses that made brainy people go forth and multiply.

I'm not saying we can completely ignore genes from now on. There have been alarming reports of the lowering of the general intelligence level because smart people have fewer babies.* If there are any genes that give people the tendency to take on memes that limit their number of offspring, they will die out in a few generations in favor of competing genes that give people a tendency to acquire childbearing memes.

So, making a note to keep an eye on our mental rearview mirror to check on the progress of genetic evolution every once in a while, let's shift into the fast lane for the rest of the book and run with the memes.

The Just-as-Selfish Meme

Understanding the evolution of memes requires quite a bit of sideways thinking. For instance, it's not useful to talk about *purpose* when it comes to evolution, as in the question "What was the evolutionary purpose of the mind?" because purpose depends on point of view.

> The mechanism of evolution has no purpose in itself; it is simply the inexorable battle of replicators for access to whatever replication mechanisms are available.

If Minerva is the name of the DNA strand that made the difference between mind and no mind, then from Minerva's point of view, the purpose of our minds is to ensure the safety and replication of Minerva. From *our* point of view, the purpose of Minerva is to give us our minds. It's a matter of perspective.

---

*One member of Mensa, the international society for people with an IQ in the top 2 percent of the population, has been known to take out the following advertisement, apparently in an attempt to preserve the fitness of whatever DNA causes high intelligence:

The smarter you are, the more children you should have.

Although an appeal like this may seem a far cry from Hitler's genocidal dream of populating the earth with a master race, there are few things more controversial than suggesting the selective breeding of human beings for any purpose whatsoever!

Instead of looking at meme evolution from our own point of view as we normally do, we need to look at it from the point of view of the meme, as if the meme were acting in its own selfish interests and doing whatever it takes to replicate and become widespread. The "selfish meme" concept does not, of course, ascribe any consciousness or motivation to the meme; it simply means we can understand better by looking at evolution from the meme's point of view.

> The evolution of ideas, culture, and society revolves around the selfish meme just as the evolution of species revolves around the selfish gene.

Again, this is not the Truth, just a useful model. And viewing life in this way may be a big pill to swallow—after all, we're used to thinking of ourselves as brilliant, freethinking individuals, not players in the meme's game—but it's a pill that relieves much of the headache of understanding how culture works.

A Meme's-Eye View

From a meme's point of view, our minds exist for the sole purpose of making copies of the meme. I'm not saying a meme *has* a point of view, just that if it did have one, that's what it would be. The selfish meme is just as selfish as the selfish gene, and the concept is just as void of any literal meaning. The only point of going through this mental pretzeling of looking at the world from the point of view of mindless replicators is that it brings a great deal of clarity to a confusing situation.

So from a meme's point of view, not only our minds and brains but also our whole bodies, cities, countries, and certainly television sets exist for that same selfish purpose. That's important to understand. If television sets did not aid in copying memes (one obvious candidate is the *Own a TV* strategy-meme), we would have no television sets! They certainly didn't evolve biologically!

> The most popular and prevalent parts of our culture are the most effective at copying memes.

Every part of our culture beyond what we see in animal cultures—and maybe even that—is a product of meme evolution. The most popular ideas are the ones that spread the easiest. The most popular art is the art with the fittest memes. Television is a crucible for meme evolution: shows that don't attract repeat viewers or word-of-mouth recommendations die quickly, replaced by an endless supply of mutations and variations. Ideas for running your business, managing your finances, and improving your life become prevalent not because they are the best for you, but because they are the *best at spreading*. The two are sometimes related, but often not.

What makes a meme good at spreading—what makes it a good replicator? We have many ways to spread memes—speech, writing, body language, monkey-see-monkey-do, television—but why do some memes, such as the proverbial bad news, travel fast . . . while other memes, such as the ones in unpopular TV shows, die quickly? We can start to get an answer to that question by speculating about the very beginnings of meme evolution, back when genetic evolution had more influence upon the contents of our brains than meme evolution did, back when natural selection picked DNA for smart brains over the alternatives.

The Purpose of Our Brains

Initially, the only purpose of our brains was to help our DNA make copies of itself. The chief way we helped it do that is by surviving, mating with other people who shared most of that DNA, and having as many children as possible live to reproduce. Originally, the purpose of our brains was one or more of the following:

- To increase our chances of surviving to the age of reproduction and beyond

- To increase the number of children we had

- To increase our chances of mating with a good mating partner, someone who would likely produce the most copies of the DNA responsible for the brain

Television sets aid in copying memes, including the *Own a TV set* meme.

In other words, our brains made us better at pursuing the four basic drives animals have, fondly referred to by zoologists as the "four F's": *fighting, fleeing, feeding,* and—er—*finding a mate.*

There were quite a few brain mechanisms already working for these drives even before the evolutionary step that gave us conscious minds. We share those mechanisms with other animals: fear, sending and receiving verbal and visual signals, memory, and an instinct for belonging to a group. All of these mechanisms aid in the replication of DNA.

The three classes I divided memes into in Chapter 2 come from some very early uses of our brains, uses that supported survival and reproduction. Even animal brains can be programmed with distinctions (a mother's face, a predator, edible food); strategies (paths to travel, ways to uncover food); and associations (memories of pleasant or dangerous experiences, of who's a friend and who's an enemy). Memes build on these basic brain functions; these brain functions are part of the "hardware design" for the software called memes.

The Evolution of Communication

As animals evolved, those that had a superior ability to communicate certain information tended to survive and reproduce better than the others. What kind of information? Back to the four F's: information about danger, about the location of food, and about the fact that they are ready to mate.

Our minds make it much easier for us to copy ideas: strategy-memes, distinction-memes, and association-memes. It's hard to overstress the importance of copying in the evolution of our culture and body of knowledge. If our minds didn't have the ability to copy ideas from each other, all of us would be limited to the knowledge we could gather for ourselves in a single lifetime.

At some point, our minds evolved to the point that we developed language. Language made meme evolution explode. It revolutionized communication by making it possible to create new concepts, new distinctions; to associate one thing with another; and to share strategies. Lower animals couldn't do that. The battle was on now for constant improvement of communication to enhance survival and reproduction.

There are two basic ways to improve communication: talk louder or listen closer. We can certainly expect natural selection to favor animals that brag verbally, visually, or otherwise about their own sexual prowess over ones that shyly wait for Mr. or Ms. Right to come along. It's a bit more difficult to see why "selfish" selection would favor a tendency to give a shout and let others know about danger or food location, but it makes sense when we realize that the "shouting" gene is probably shared among the shouter and the listeners. Remember that genetic evolution selects for *genes,* not individuals.

On the listening end, natural selection will tend to choose an animal that's ready to drop everything and pay attention to important information over another with a tendency to ignore it. From a gene's point of view, important information is whatever will protect, and increase the number of copies of, that gene—that is, information about danger, food, and sex. If Bambi's mom had pricked up her ears just a touch sooner, she might be alive today to tell her story of how she heard the twig breaking under the hunter's boot in just the nick of time.*

Communication evolved in order to communicate very specific things: danger, food, and sex. Therefore, we, as the product of the evolution of animals, find ourselves with the tendency both to talk about and to pay attention to danger, food, and sex in preference to other subjects.

> Memes involving danger, food, and sex spread faster than other memes because we are wired to pay more attention to them—we have *buttons* around those subjects.

The Origin of Memes

What were the original memes so important to our survival and reproduction that communicating humans proliferated? We can imagine:

— **Crisis.** The quick spreading of fear saved many lives by alerting people quickly to danger. We see nonconscious animals exhibit communication of the *crisis* meme—for example, in

---

*Deer, of course, haven't had much time to adapt to the recent invention of firearms, but generations from now we should not be surprised to see most deer with color vision; thick hides; or even ugly, misshapen heads that no one would want for a trophy. Already in parts of the southwestern United States, the most common variety of rattlesnake is silent: it rears up and shakes its tail as usual, but no sound comes out. Rattling out loud, it seems, gets you shot.

stampedes—but communication of the distinction-meme *crisis* along with specific details had more survival value.

— **Mission.** Communicating a mission such as fighting an enemy, building shelter, or finding food allowed people to survive in times of adversity or scarcity. Groups of people who evolved to be good at sending and receiving the *mission* meme had fitter DNA than those who were not, because they were able to work together for a common goal.

— **Problem.** Identifying a situation—such as lack of food, competition for potential mates, and so on—as a problem to be solved made each individual better equipped to survive and mate.

— **Danger.** In particular, knowledge about potential dangers, even if not immediate crises, was valuable. Knowing where predators hunted or where water was poisoned enhanced survival.

— **Opportunity.** Acting quickly to avoid missing out on a reward—historically, food, prey, or a potential mate—that presented itself was of benefit to evolving humans.

All of these memes are very much with us today. It would be surprising if they were not, since, on a DNA-evolutionary scale, it was just recently that our brains evolved to give us consciousness and thereby the ability to communicate memes on a large scale. But it would be a challenge to find any culture or subculture on Earth today that did not concern itself with crises, missions, problems, dangers, or opportunities, although there may be great disagreement over the nature of those.

Let's run a quick check to see if we spend an inordinate amount of our communication bandwidth on those subjects, sprinkled in with our old friends danger, food, and sex: Flip through a few channels on your TV. Leaf through a few pages of your daily newspaper. As I write this, the national fiction bestseller list is populated with thrillers and love stories; and the nonfiction list has books about deadly diseases (viruses!), improving your sex life, eating better food, and political crises, with only the occasional self-improvement book to offer a twinkle of hope. And people probably only read *those* because they're scared of the danger they'll encounter if they don't! I always thought the book *The Doctor's Quick Weight Loss Diet* must have sold a million copies on the memes in the title alone. What an *opportunity* to have someone you *trust* address the *problem* of your *sex-appeal crisis* over *food!*

To illustrate the effectiveness of the *crisis, mission, problem, danger,* and *opportunity* memes, read the following two paragraphs, both accurate descriptions of a book about memes. The first paragraph doesn't have these memes in it:

> *Introduction to Memetics* is a compilation of ideas on the science of memetics. Each chapter summarizes a different topic in this field. Included are examples of how memetics impacts people's lives, illustrates historical data, and offers choices for the future.

The second is chock-full of all five of these key memes:

> *Virus of the Mind* exposes the imminent crisis of the dangerous new technology known as *memetics.* What is it, and how can we guard against its harmful effects? Our only chance is to have everyone read *Virus of the Mind* before it is too late!

A common reaction would be to fall asleep halfway through the first paragraph and to pay much more attention to the second. You have little control over that tendency: your brain is hardwired to respond that way. You may have noticed some *skepticism* kicking in while reading the second paragraph. The *skepticism* strategy-meme protects the existing set of memes your mind is holding to some degree. Unfortunately, it resists beneficial and harmful memes equally.

Pushing Our Buttons

Now it gets more complicated, so hold on tight. Remember, our brains were not engineered for a specific purpose; they were "kluged" together by natural selection, different things being tried out, strengthened, weakened, and combined, until something interesting happened that caused the genes responsible for that thing to replicate better than the others.

That's how our brains, and those of other animals, evolved to pay close attention to information involving danger, food, and sex. And when meme evolution started to take off, the memes that initially succeeded were ones involving danger, food, and sex, among others. Among others? Sure, because our brains have a natural tendency to pay attention to some other things, too. Laughter and yawning, for instance, are both contagious—our brains tend to replicate them when they're around.

But most of the things to which our brains are attentive evolved in order to support our survival and reproduction. The complexity comes because genetic evolution didn't just stop at the point where we were equipped to notice a tiger running toward us, a ready-to-eat meal, or an eyelash-batting member of the opposite sex.

> Evolution naturally progressed to select for a diversity of clever, sneaky, and indirect ways of avoiding danger, finding food, and wooing mates.

Before consciousness, we had no way of coming about these strategies logically or rationally, but we did have feelings, instincts, and drives, as we suspect other animals do, too.

All animals have four basic instinctual drives: fighting, fleeing, feeding, and mating. So in addition to paying attention to danger, food, and sex, our brains come equipped with two ways of dealing with danger and one each for food and sex, with no conscious thought necessary. These drives work by firing up appropriate parts of our brains, which, if we don't consciously intervene, will drive us to satisfy the need. Even if we do consciously refrain from acting on impulse, we can feel this all going on quite easily and in fact have names for the distinct feelings that go along with the drives to fight, flee, feed, and mate: *anger, fear, hunger,* and *lust.*

These four feelings are wired so directly into our brains that, civilized though we may get, we experience from time to time something or someone "pushing our buttons"—saying or doing something that generates one of these basic feelings in us. The phrase is usually associated with anger, but we've got buttons for fear, hunger, and lust that are just as big and just as pushable. As civilized human beings, of course, we know we don't have to give in to impulse and *act* when our buttons are pushed, but it's very, very difficult to avoid *paying attention* when it happens. And where there's attention, there are memes.

The idea of paying attention plays a central role in understanding memes. A meme that lots of people pay attention to will be more successful than a meme that few notice. So over the millions of years necessary for major genetic evolution to take place, we aren't surprised to find that most animals, including ourselves, have a genetic tendency to pay attention to the things that were important in getting us where we are today: danger, food, and sex.

In our search for mind viruses, then, our first candidates will be situations that push one or more of these four buttons—anger, fear, hunger, and lust—and thus draw our attention, our precious attention, to a use of our consciousness for which, upon reflection, we would not choose to spend it.

Consciousness

Enhanced communication had huge survival value in the evolution of human beings. But the innovation that makes us human is *consciousness*. It's the same innovation that makes us such a wonderful environment for meme evolution. Initially, consciousness must have served the same purpose as all these other brain mechanisms: helping our DNA make copies of itself through our survival and reproduction. How did consciousness assist? It's not difficult to speculate. Here are a few ideas:

- It allowed better communication and cooperation between people for finding food and for self-defense.

- It allowed planning for the future.

- Problem-solving ability made it easier to find food and mates.

- A greater ability to understand the world led to increased success in all aspects of life.

It's important to understand what the brain's priorities are, because our thoughts are naturally biased toward these things.

> The deep thoughts we think and the elegant intellectual models we build are all kluged on top of these advanced survival and mating functions of the brain, which in turn are kluged on top of the primitive survival and mating functions—fear, anger, hunger, and lust.

Second-Order Buttons

Did genetic evolution stop there, with those four basic drives? No, evolution continued. Our brains evolved countless secondary strategies to make us better not only at survival and reproduction, but also at satisfying those four first-order urges. Here are a few second-order instinctual drives some people seem to have that are all opportunities for memes to take advantage of:

— **Belonging.** Humans are gregarious—that is, they like company. There are any number of evolutionary reasons for the existence of this drive, including safety in numbers, economies of scale, and simply the presence of more potential mates. Memes that give people a feeling of belonging to a group have an advantage over memes that don't.

— **Distinguishing yourself.** A drive to do something new, innovative, or significant makes an individual more likely to find food or shelter and makes him stand out from the crowd as a potential mate. Any memes that make people feel distinguished, special, or important have an edge in meme evolution.

— **Caring.** Since humans share the great majority of their DNA with all other humans, it makes sense that we evolved a drive to care about the welfare of other people.* Memes that take advantage of people's caring natures have an advantage in the battle for a share of our minds.

— **Approval.** A drive to do what others, or you yourself, approve of. As animals and humans evolved into societies, individuals fulfilling whatever their roles were did a better job of perpetuating their genes, and presumably the genes shared by others in their community, than those who didn't play by the rules. Successful memes hook into people's drive to get approval and play on the guilt, shame, and hurt that result if they don't get it.

— **Obeying authority.** It was in an individual's genetic interest —that is, in the interest of his DNA—to recognize the authority of someone more powerful or wiser than he is. Going along with that authority would increase his DNA's chance of survival and replication, while fighting the authority might get him killed or left out in the cold.

---

*In fact, since we share a lot of DNA with mammals, it makes sense that we care about *them*. It would be interesting to see a study correlating how much people care about various animal species with how much DNA those species have in common with humans. I bet dogs and cats would beat out chimps, though, despite the fact that chimps share more DNA with us. Why? See p. 168.

The way these second-order drives work is similar to the way the primary drives work: you get some kind of *good feeling* when you're doing the thing that the drive drives you to do, or you get a *bad feeling* when you're not. These second-order feelings often aren't as clear-cut as anger, fear, hunger, and lust; and we don't even know if everybody has the same kinds of feelings for the same kinds of drives. Nevertheless, people who have the drive to belong, or the drive to distinguish themselves, know what I'm talking about. The important point is:

> People have many secondary drives connected to various strong feelings, and memes that activate these feelings have the evolutionary advantage.

We will simply pay more attention to memes that push our buttons because that is our nature. Our tendency to pay special attention to these memes makes them more likely to replicate and become embedded in our culture. Memes that push our primary and secondary buttons have an evolutionary advantage over memes that don't, even if those other memes might be more accurate or more supportive of our quality of life. Remember: *quality* of life is not what natural selection is about; *quantity* of replication is.

Just as DNA replicates when the organism it generates survives and reproduces, memes replicate when the behavior they cause attracts attention. Pushing our buttons is a great way to attract attention to a meme, so memes that annoy, seduce, enrage, or scare us tend to become widespread.

More Fit Memes

Meme evolution happened—and continues to happen—fast. Practically the instant we became capable of copying memes, they started to evolve. They evolved away from those basic types that our brains were designed to spread and toward ones that for whatever reason were better at spreading—were fitter memes. Memes evolved through cultural "organisms" in the environment of the society of human minds, just as DNA evolved through organisms in the environment of the earth.

In addition to the survival-oriented memes that are still with us, there are some more types of memes that don't seem to particularly help or hurt our survival, but by their very nature are fit to spread effectively—these are memes that are fit simply because they are variations on the idea *Spread this meme:*

— **Tradition.** A strategy-meme to continue what was done or believed in the past is automatically self-perpetuating. It doesn't matter whether the tradition is good or bad, important or irrelevant. Say you have two adult service clubs, the Kangaroo Club and the Slug Club. The Slug charter stresses tradition—conducting meetings on Saturday mornings, employing a little ritual of emptying the saltshakers before lunch, and so on; the Kangaroo charter stresses novelty and variety. In 20 years, the Slugs' *tradition* meme is still likely to be around, carrying with it the *Meet Saturday morning* meme and the *Empty saltshaker* meme. The Kangaroos' original memes will have died in the name of variety.

Once a tradition gets started, it automatically continues until something more powerful stops it. People infected with *tradition* memes are programmed to *"repeat* this meme in the future and *spread this meme* to future generations!" Traditions die hard.

— **Evangelism.** Any meme that explicitly involves spreading itself to other people has an added advantage over other memes. Evangelism is often combined with the *mission* meme, making it even more powerful. It makes little difference whether the thing being evangelized is true or false, good or bad; evangelism works so well that it has become one of the most prevalent memes on Earth. Evangelism tells us to *"spread this meme* as much as you can!"

Then there are memes that become entrenched in people's minds and are extremely resistant to attack:

— **Faith.** Any meme that entails believing in it blindly can never be dislodged from your belief system by any attack or argument. Combined with *evangelism, faith* makes for a powerful mind-virus envelope that can be stuffed with just about any content.

— **Skepticism.** Questioning new ideas is a defense against new memes. The opposite of *faith, skepticism* actually has a very similar effect on the mind programmed with it. Skeptics are resistant to new ideas just as the faithful are. A faithful and a skeptic can argue forever and never learn anything.

Other memes are fit because of the nature of communication. Imagine a group of people playing the game of "telephone." One player starts by whispering a sentence in the next player's ear. That player whispers whatever she hears to the next player, who continues the process until the message, usually garbled beyond recognition, finally makes its way back to the originator, who bursts out laughing at the way his message has evolved. This is meme evolution in a microcosm! What kinds of memes survive the ordeal?

— **Familiarity.** Unusual words or phrases quickly metamorphose into familiar ones: *"pâté de foie gras"* might quickly become "putty defogger" in one game. The familiar spreads more quickly than the unfamiliar because people have distinction-memes for familiar things already and therefore notice them more.

— **Making sense.** Memes that make sense spread more quickly than ones that don't. People are quick to accept flawed explanations that make more sense over more accurate ones that are harder to understand. You see this happen all the time when famous quotations get distorted through evolution: does music have charms that soothe the savage *beast* or *breast?* Playwright William Congreve said the latter.

My favorite example of meme evolution through the universal game of "telephone" is Emerson's quotation from his essay *Self-*

Reliance: "A foolish consistency is the hobgoblin of little minds." This one gets mangled so much that I even have a book, about quotations and facts commonly misquoted, that *misquotes Emerson in its supposed correction!*

Emerson's quote points out the danger of falling into the *Truth Trap.* The hobgoblin of little minds—what keeps people from making the most of their lives—is allowing the random memetic programming you got since you were born to direct your life consistent with itself. Understanding memetics gives you a chance to look inside at what programs you are running and, if you choose, to reprogram yourself powerfully and consciously to point your life in whatever direction you desire.

Of course, then you have to look at what programs are governing your evaluation of how you're programmed, at what programs are governing what you think you desire, then at what programs are governing your motives for reprogramming yourself, and . . . ! Soon you find yourself deep into the realm of philosophy. The science of memetics does not carry with it a value judgment of how you *should* live your life; it just gives you a lot of power over living it however you choose. Consciously.

The theory of memetics—the *memetics* metamemes—although invented decades ago, has had difficulty spreading. In writing *Virus of the Mind,* I have the goal of packaging as many fit memes as possible with the *memetics* metameme so that it will spread as quickly and widely as possible. Doesn't that make sense?

Old Brain, New World

Memetics is not the only scientific idea that isn't widely known. Many such ideas are difficult for people to grasp. In fact, science, including memetics, is just one aspect of modern culture

---

1,001 Facts Somebody Screwed Up by Deane Jordan (Longstreet Press, 1993). The author embarrassingly states: "Emerson—Ralph Waldo—did not say, 'Inconsistency is the hobgoblin of little minds.' He said, 'A foolish inconsistency is the hobgoblin of little minds.' Big difference." Yep.

that our brains are ill equipped to understand. But why would we expect our brains to be good at dealing with modern culture? Would we expect a computer to "understand" its own program? No! It just needs to *run* the program, not understand it. And our brains evolved not to understand themselves, but to perform very specific tasks. It takes a lot of hard work for people to use those brains, which were not designed for that purpose, to understand science!

The "wiring" in our brains evolved over millions of years. During that time, our environment changed very little, as we can verify by examining archaeological digs. It is only very, very recently in the timescale of genetic evolution that our environment started to change so fast that day-to-day routines could be altered significantly within a single lifetime. To understand memes, we need to realize that our brains, which evolved to support our survival in a relatively unchanging world, remain essentially the same even though we have transformed our world many times over since we evolved to the point of consciousness.

Meme evolution selects for the ideas, beliefs, attitudes, and myths that we pay the most attention to and broadcast the loudest. And *without conscious intervention,* what we pay attention to and broadcast the loudest is determined by that complex web of feelings and drives, cravings and fears, that evolved to keep us alive and mating.

The word *pay* in "pay attention" is quite apt. As we are conscious beings, attention is our most precious commodity. Attention is a piece of our consciousness, a slice of our human life. When we direct our attention at something, we are spending a piece of our conscious life. How many of us consciously direct our attention toward whatever is most important to us? I for one hate the fact that my attention tends to get sucked in by people and events that push my survive-and-reproduce buttons, relics of my animal past. Those buttons make me unconsciously waste large portions of my life.

The point is that danger, food, and sex are the priorities of your *genes,* not necessarily your own personal priorities. When you feel your attention being pulled away from what is most important to you by an apparent crisis, the latest and greatest pizza from Domino's, or an attractive passerby, your genes are conspiring to steal your most valuable possession: your consciousness.

Ideas are infectious. We catch them from other people's behavior, from the little bits of culture all around us. That's great if the ideas we catch are good ideas—ones that help us with whatever we're up to in life. The problem is, as you've just seen, ideas spread according to how good their memes are, not so much according to how useful they are to our lives or even according to how true they are.

> As nice as it might be to imagine that we are evolving toward a better, more civilized, more compassionate world, what we're really evolving toward is a world full of memes and mind viruses that replicate better.

Ever wonder why life can be such a struggle sometimes? There's a fantasy people have that an ideal life would mean just relaxing and doing what comes naturally. Well, I hate to be the one to break the bad news, but *what comes naturally* is so far removed from our modern life as to be irrelevant. Because of the speedy evolution of culture, technology, and society, we can't even say anymore that *what comes naturally* leads us to replicate as many copies as possible of our genes. Today, *what comes naturally* is a horrendous mismatch between the old wiring of our brains for prehistoric times and the completely different challenges and opportunities of the modern world.

Our brains are still wired to pay attention to, and generate feelings for, situations that were important to us in prehistoric times—and important *only* in the sense that they helped our genes make as many copies of themselves as possible. The ideas that spread the easiest, and therefore pervade society, are the ones that easily penetrate that old Stone Age brain of ours. The whole of science has been a concerted effort to *foil* that natural selection of Stone Age ideas by our brains and instead select ideas that are useful, that work, that are accurate models of reality. But science is way ahead of the rest of culture in that sense.

In the Long Run

Now wait a minute. Memes are an evolutionary adaptation of human beings. Doesn't that mean that, whatever madness there is in their methods, we can be certain that memes have our best interests at heart? Aren't we guaranteed that, eventually, they will contribute to our becoming better and better adapted to our environment? In the long run, whatever goes on with this meme business, we'll land on our feet, because, well, species just adapt automatically to whatever the environment throws at them. Don't they?

It would be nice to think that, but it won't happen that way unless the way evolution handles it is to eliminate memes altogether, and us along with them. Memes have their own evolutionary path. They *do not* evolve to support the replication of our genes. If you don't believe me, look at the fact that the cultures we consider most advanced have the smallest population growth but the most effective cultural imperialism. They're spreading memes, not genes.

Okay, so meme evolution won't automatically contribute to our sex lives or our family size. But at least it will contribute to our survival, won't it? In the long run? Doesn't it have to? After all, memes *live* in our minds, don't they?

Nope. As we speak, information is finding more and more ways to replicate and survive. Ideas that would once be forgotten without a trace are now available instantly through information-retrieval systems. Computers now back themselves up automatically, replicating all the information in themselves. The e-mail chain letter is an early example of a virus hosted by both computers and minds.*

---

*The evolution of chain letters is an interesting study in itself. A recent posting on Internet computer bulletin boards warned there was a message going around that you *should not read* because it contained a virus. Naturally, the author requested that people copy and repost the warning so as to protect others from the danger. Thoughtful Net users wondered just how a message could contain a computer virus—computers need to run a program to get infected with a virus, not simply display text. But for a week or so, copies of the warning message were everywhere! Which electronic message contained the virus?

As computers get smarter, computer-based replicators will become common—mutating replicators that not only spread but also evolve. And as computer-based replicators start to overtake mind-based memes as the primary repositories and communicators of information, these new replicators could have more influence on the shape of the world than memes do, just as memes overtook DNA as shapers of the global environment. Maybe non-human-based replicators will evolve to the point where we fade into the background, mere asterisks in the stat book of the universe! And if we should start getting in the way of these new computer-based replicators, as so many species of DNA-based replicators have gotten in our way and become endangered or extinct, then—?!

If we do survive, what about our quality of life? Is it evolving for better or worse? Some might intuitively feel that if we just let cultural evolution run its natural course, all the competing political, religious, commercial, and scientific ideas will eventually melt together in a kind of free-enterprise system of the mind and evolve into a utopian state, a return to Eden or arrival at Nirvana. This was the idea behind social Darwinism, a popular political philosophy in the days of the robber barons.

On the other hand, we might look at the fact that meme evolution happens with lightning speed compared to the genetic evolution of human beings and conclude that, unchecked, meme evolution will have us devote more and more of our mental resources to replicating memes. We might worry that more and more effective mind viruses will evolve and leave us as unsuspecting and unhappy hosts, our lives devoted to their service. Supposing such mind viruses grudgingly keep us alive and communicating, they still have no requirement to help us enjoy life or even keep us free from pain. The mass of men would lead lives of quiet desperation.

Where is meme evolution taking us? Nirvana? A living hell? Nowhere in particular? Is there anything we can do to direct it? If there is, should we?

Subject: FAST CASH
From: Anonymous

Follow these instructions EXACTLY, and in 20 to 60 days you will have received over 50,000.00 dollars IN CASH.

[1] Immediately mail $1.00 to the first 5 names listed below, starting at number 1 through number 5. SEND CASH ONLY. (Total investment: $5.00) Enclose a note with each letter stating: "Please add my name to your mailing list". Include your name and mailing address. (This is a legitimate service that you are requesting and you are paying $1.00 for this service.)

[2] Remove the name that appears as number 1 on the list. Move the other 9 names up one position (Number 2 becomes number 1, number 3 becomes number 2, and so on). Place your name, address, and zip code in the number 10 position.

[3] With your name in the number 10 position, upload this ENTIRE file to 15 (Fifteen) different bulletin boards. You may post it to the BBS's message base or to the file section. Name it FASTCASH.TXT, and use the file description comments to draw attention to this file and its great potential for all of us.

[4] Within 60 days you will receive over $50,000.00 in CASH.
Keep a copy of this file for yourself so that you can use it again and again whenever you need money. As soon as you mail out these letters you are automatically in the mail order business. People will be sending YOU $1.00 to be placed on your mailing list. This list can then be rented to a broker that can be found in your local yellow pages listings for additional income on a regular basis. The list will become more valuable as it grows in size.

NOTE: Make sure that you retain EVERY name and address sent to you, either on computer or hard copy, but do not discard the names and notes that people send to you. This is PROOF that you are truly providing a service, and should the IRS or some other government agency question you, you can provide them with this proof!

Remember, as each post is downloaded and the instructions carefully followed, five members will be reimbursed for their participation as List Developer with $1.00 each. Your name will move up the list geometrically so that when your name reaches the number 5 position you will be receiving thousands of dollars in cash. REMEMBER - THIS PROGRAM FAILS ONLY IF YOU ARE NOT HONEST - PLEASE!! PLEASE BE HONORABLE...IT DOES WORK! THANK YOU.

[list of names deleted]

The following letter was written by a participating member in this program.
****
To those with the COMMON sense to participate in this easy money opportunity: About six months ago I received the enclosed post in letter form. I ignored it. I received about five more of the same letter within the next two week. I ignored them also. Of course, I was tempted to follow through and dreamed of making thousands, but I was convinced it was just another gimmick and could not possibly work. I was wrong! About three weeks later I saw this same letter posted on a local bulletin board in Montreal. I liked the idea of giving it a try with my computer. I didn't expect much because I figured, if other people were as skeptical as I, they would not be too quick to part with $5.00. But, I BUY LOTTERY TICKETS WEEKLY IN MY PROVINCE AND HAVE NOTHING TO SHOW FOR IT BUT TICKET STUBS! This week I decided to look at this as my weekly lottery purchase. I addressed the envelopes and mailed out $1.00 in each as directed. Two weeks went by and I didn't receive anything in the mail. The fourth week rolled around and I couldn't believe what happened! I can not say that I received $50,000.00, but it was definitely well over $35,000.00! For the first time in 10 years I got out of debt. It was great. Of course, it did not take me long to go through my earnings, so I am using this excellent money making opportunity once again. FOLLOW THE INSTRUCTIONS AND GET READY TO ENJOY! Please send a copy of this letter along with the enclosed letter so together we can convince people who are skeptical that this really does work!

One persistent Internet electronic chain letter is an example of a replicator hosted by both computers and minds.

One key to answering these questions lies in the controversial new field of *evolutionary psychology*—the study of how and why our minds evolved to be the way they are today. We already started to explore evolutionary psychology in the discussion of our four basic drives and the nature of communication. Now let's take a detailed look at the subject that forms the core of evolutionary psychology and eternally one of our favorite topics: sex.

CHAPTER SIX

SEX:
THE ROOT OF
ALL EVOLUTION

*"Science is a lot like sex. Sometimes something useful
comes of it, but that's not the reason we're doing it."*

— Richard Feynman

The most fascinating discovery of the new field of evolutionary psychology is the central role that sex plays, and has played, in
shaping our modern behavior and culture. Weaving a twisted path
connecting Freud, male chauvinism, puritanism, and womaniz-
ing, evolutionary psychology explains the complexity and contra-
diction inherent in human behavior as never before.

As you read this, remember: evolutionary psychology is
about tendencies—predispositions and historical artifacts of evolution. It may be true that men are from Mars and women are
from Venus, but that doesn't mean we have to live there. People
are completely capable of growing in any direction they choose.
What you're about to read is neither a fatalistic preordainment of
people's futures nor an excuse for behaving like an animal. It's just
interesting to know how we got where we are today. And we got
here, every one of us, as the result of successful matings.

This is the obvious insight, the seed out of which grows this whole beautiful new theory:

> You are the result of an unbroken chain spanning thousands of generations of males and females who were *all* successful at finding a mate.

When we look at it that way, is it any wonder that our sex drives are so strong? That people are willing to lie, cheat, and steal for sex? That U.S. senators risk and lose their careers rather than pass up an opportunity to have sex with a teenage page? That women stay in abusive relationships rather than lose the potential protector of their children? As bad as these decisions seem if we think about them purely rationally, we make them anyway because of our tremendously strong genetic tendencies relating to sex.

Over and over again, since the beginning of sexual reproduction, genes that gave people—and animals before them—a mating edge over their peers were the ones that got passed down. Likewise, natural selection was unforgiving of individuals who, by choice or destiny, failed to mate successfully. Their DNA died with them.

The Battle for Sex

The battle for sex was the prime fighting ground in the war of DNA to copy itself. For any sexually reproducing creatures, including us, natural selection worked with incredible speed to wipe out any DNA that made its host less likely to have children and to reinforce any DNA that increased its host's probability of reproducing.

There are innumerable ways in which DNA can influence its host's success in mating, but the most straightforward is to enhance whatever appeals to the opposite sex: accentuate the positive and eliminate the negative. Since the most attractive individuals will reproduce more than the rest, we would expect attractiveness to be selected for—not simply good looks, but every quality that appeals to the opposite sex.

> As a result of genetic evolution, individuals evolve to be more and more sexually attractive.

Well, isn't that nice! Doesn't that just give you a smug, complacent feeling? It's about time something good came out of this evolution business. You can just sit back and watch, and look forward to an endlessly increasing supply of potential mates! Ahh. If you want, just put this book down for a while and daydream. Life is good.

Unfortunately, though, what is true for the human race as a whole is not true for every individual man or woman. Although the species may be evolving wondrously, we just get the DNA we're dealt and make do with it. And make do we do! The industries that have sprung up in order to enhance people's sexual attraction (and attractiveness) are enormous: fashion, cosmetics, diet programs, and fitness clubs are just a few of the cultural institutions that have emerged to feed people's drive to be more appealing. Short of replacing our current system of reproducing with test tubes and cloning, we're stuck with it: sexual reproduction is where survival of the fittest (genes) gets down to the nitty-gritty.

So like it or not, many of the genetic tendencies we are born with revolve around sex and mating. Let's take a step back now and see how genetic evolution got us where we are today. This is all speculation, since we don't have much historical data about how people behaved in prehistoric times, but it all falls out from understanding the selfish-gene concept.

Sex: The Early Days

Imagine it's the early days of sexual reproduction in animals. Males and females pretty much mate with each other at random, with whomever is convenient. In fact, males attempt to mate with other males, and females with other females, having not yet figured out how to tell the difference. (I said these were the early days.) In fact, they're mating with rocks, trees, mushrooms, other species—whatever they can find. It's very much like the way plant spores and pollen blow about in the wind, most of the seed being spilled, but a bit falling in just the right place on the female plant for fertilization to occur. It's not a particularly efficient system, but it works.

Over the course of time, the genes of the animals that tend to be a bit more discriminating in their choice of mates—passing up the rocks, trees, and other species—tend to be a bit more successful in replicating themselves. So animals evolve to be more discriminating. How do they do it? Remember, this is not a conscious process or even a process of ever-improving design. It's a random process of kluge upon kluge. Suppose one species has developed a keen sense of smell as an adaptation against predators. The individuals that use that sense of smell to tell the difference between members of their own species and rocks have the advantage. Pretty soon, the species evolves toward using its sense of smell to discern mates, although its members still can't tell the difference between males and females.

Now suppose it turns out that females have a hormone that males don't have, and there's a discernible odor produced by that hormone for no particular reason, but one that males can smell. The males that tend to use that information to be picky about their mates are more successful than the ones who simply ignore it, and pretty soon the animals evolve to be even more discriminating.

This step-by-step, inch-by-inch process continues constantly, the more discerning males having better success at reproduction and therefore filling the gene pool with more copies of their DNA than the others.

Okay, let's look at the female end. Now that the gene pool is filled with sniffing connoisseurs of female odors, any females that tend to produce *more* of that odor have the advantage in attracting mates over the rest. At this point, males will start evolving to pick up on other differences between males and females: coloration, size, shape—*vive la différence!* The more discerning males will be more successful, and the females that accentuate those features will also be more successful. This brings us back to where we started the discussion, with individuals evolving to be more and more sexually attractive.

This works in the other direction, too: females can require stricter and stricter standards for their mates, so long as they are physically able to resist their advances. It's common among birds to see males with brilliant plumage courting dull females; in these cases the females evolved to be more discriminating, and the males evolved to have more and more pronounced sex characteristics.

It's important to remember that this evolution of sex characteristics is not happening by plan or design, just by the interaction between the chaotic force of random variation and the organizing force of evolution. Like a self-winding watch, evolution harnesses the disorganized movements and changes in the environment to make slow but steady progress, the ratchet locking the winding gear's motion in the forward direction, through the course of the eons.

One way in which evolution happened to make progress was by specializing the roles of males and females, a distinction known as *sexual differentiation*. Evolutionary psychology shows that there really are significant differences in men's and women's drives and tendencies—in general. When these differences become stereotyped and used as weapons against individuals, we use a less-kind term: *sexism*.

The Origin of Sexism

The psychological differences between men and women began when mammals evolved to put all their eggs in one basket, so to speak: inside the female. Actually, sexual differentiation started even earlier than that, practically at the origin of sex, when females evolved to produce big, relatively expensive ova and males evolved to produce small, cheap sperm. The splitting apart of the behavior of males and females stems from the fact that female DNA has a big commitment to and investment in each fertilized egg, while male DNA has nothing to lose and everything to gain by giving its host the tendency to fertilize every female in sight, then prowl around looking for the ones that aren't in sight.

If this sounds like a shallow caricature or an Andy Capp comic strip, remember: we inherited many of our drives and tendencies from animals and prehistoric humans, before concepts such as marriage and monogamy arrived. The DNA of males who mated with only one female had a terrible disadvantage: the other males who were going around spreading their DNA as widely as possible were going to have a lot more children. Without considering any other factors, males evolved to reproduce as much as possible. Remember: it's all about DNA.

Females, on the other hand, having only a few chances per lifetime to pass on their DNA and many eager suitors, evolved to be a bit more selective. How did they select? A couple of factors were important. First, they wanted a male with "good" DNA, whatever that means. It might have meant a strong, healthy body, which would be passed on to the offspring and give them a better shot at survival. It might have meant having certain DNA in common with them, as evidenced by similar body features or behavior, since that doubled the chances that the offspring would carry that DNA.

Second, they wanted a mate who would invest his time and resources in the children while they were immature and vulnerable, thus increasing their chance of survival. It wasn't essential, of course, that the genetic father be the one who sticks around and raises the kids; in fact, an ideal situation for a prehistoric female might have been to have a he-man type with good genes as the biological father and a househusband type who's willing to raise the kids, if she could trick the guy into doing it somehow.

Now it was the males' turn to fight back. Given the priorities of females, males evolved in one of two directions: either becoming stronger and more handsome, or becoming a convincing potential husband and father. While both would benefit from having as much sex as possible, the he-men could be a lot more overt about it, even physically overpowering unwilling females, since their off-spring had a better chance of survival even without them sticking around. The househusband types, however, evolved to become good at finding a female who wasn't going to cheat on them. They might even prefer less-attractive females, or at least females who are less attractive to the he-man type, to increase their chances of being the biological father. They still wanted to have as much sex as possible but needed to be a bit more surreptitious—the big, strong he-men weren't going to take the competition lying down, and the females weren't particularly thrilled with having a mate who was already committed to someone else.

Time-out!

Time for two reminders:

1. I'm talking about general tendencies in evolution, not about specific individuals. Specific individuals may have *niche strategies,* which I'll discuss later in the chapter. Not everybody is like this! People behave differently and are attracted to different types of mates, in different circumstances. And what about homosexuals? (There's no agreement among scientists about how evolution could produce homosexuals, but I'll hazard a guess later in the chapter.)

2. All this happens *unconsciously.* No doubt people tend to read this chapter and, about once a page, say to themselves, "That's ridiculous! I don't think like that! She doesn't think like that! He doesn't think like that!"

> This is not about thinking. All this clever, klugy process of mate selection happens unconsciously. The result of the unconscious calculation is that you have *feelings of attraction* for someone.

Of course, if having certain thoughts increased your chances of mating, evolution would have selected for your having those thoughts. There is nothing in the universe as complicated as this process of sexual selection, which has evolved over millions of generations to incorporate every kluge that came along.

Back to the Evolution of Sex

The eons pass, and the pivotal role of sex in evolution causes things to get more and more complicated and involved. These two roles—he-man and househusband—split off into many sub-roles, with male dominance hierarchies, female territorial disputes, and all manner of deceit and subterfuge becoming more and more prevalent for one and only one reason: it works. The behaviors that evolved around sex, up until the very recent past when memes appeared on the scene, did so because that's what got DNA passed down. In the harsh reality of genetic evolution, there was no concern for love, sensitivity, or fairness; the only thing that mattered was how many children you had—children who themselves grew up to reproduce.

Now here's the next bombshell. A common paradigm people have about life places sex as a small, if confusing, part of a grand culture based on values, morals, traditions, and God-given rights.

> Viewed through memetics, all values, morals, traditions, and ideas with respect to God and rights are the result of meme evolution. And meme evolution is guided by our genetic tendencies, which in turn evolved around sex.

The male-dominated hierarchical system, sometimes called the *patriarchy,* is a perfect example. Some feminist writers have cautioned women against buying into this system, and with good reason: the whole thing evolved so that the DNA of males could be passed down most efficiently. Is that any way to design an economy?

Why are men so obsessed with dominance relationships, with who's above and below them on the power ladder? The best theory is that it was an adaptation to establish which males had sexual rights to which women without constantly fighting about it, which didn't do anybody any good. Because of that, males seem to have a sixth sense that tells them what their position is relative to other males in any situation. The typical female sense of status is based more on attractiveness or popularity than dominance.

Most businesses, the government, the military, and even the Catholic Church are set up as overt hierarchies—it's explicitly clear who reports to whom, and who takes and gives orders. On the surface of it, these organizational hierarchies now have little to do with access to females, but the behavior and feelings men have in them are still the same. Making the hierarchy explicit avoids many face-to-face battles for position; however, it can be extremely frustrating for men with brains evolved to do whatever they can to rise in the hierarchy—to have access to more and better females—but who see no way to improve their position.

But wait a minute—don't some men (and women) like power for its own sake? Don't they enjoy the control it gives them over their destiny, the freedom to live their lives, and—well, just the *power rush?* Yes, that's all true. But the *reason* that power is such a rush is that we have evolved to have wiring in our brains that makes us crave that power.

> Through the course of evolution, the men who enjoyed and hungered for power, for a top rung in the dominance hierarchy, pushed harder for it and therefore *got more mates!*

Not only did they get more mates, but they also got more resources to give to their children, enhancing *their* chances of reproducing. The most unforgiving force in genetic evolution—sexual reproduction—screened out those males who *didn't* enjoy power. They didn't reproduce nearly as much, their children didn't have as good a chance of reproducing, and their genes faded away as the genes responsible for the power lust grew more and more prevalent. Men don't consciously think, *Gee, I'd better seek and display power so I can manipulate women into mating with me.* Evolution has made them seek and display power instinctively.

The Civilizing Effect of Women

Throughout history, while males have been pushing culture in the direction of expansion, conquest, and increased power, females have been the so-called civilizing force, striving for security and safety. These drives are direct offshoots of the different priorities of the male and female genes: males' genes tend to win by encouraging their hosts to mate with as many females as possible, while females' genes tend to win by giving their hosts the tendency to create a safe and secure environment to raise the children.

Why? Because males had relatively little investment of their time and energy in a particular fetus, while females couldn't produce more than one a year or so and needed to protect their genetic capital. Did males have an investment in any given child surviving to reproduce? You bet. Was their investment as great as a female's? Not if they were high enough on the dominance hierarchy that they could impregnate a whole bunch of women. And those men were the ones who passed down the most genes. So it fell to the females, in order to protect their investment, to set certain standards for acceptable male behavior.

> Because women's genes had more to gain by being picky about mates, evolution made women the ones who usually chose from among suitors. Men had to compete to be chosen.

So women could afford to be selective, much more so than men. They could afford to put men through some tests to see if they were serious about the relationship. By holding out until a man invested a substantial amount of time and resources, they lessened the possibility that their suitor was merely toying with their affections. They increased the probability that the guy was indeed playing the husband/father role and not just looking for some cheap thrills.

If all this sounds hopelessly cold and calculating, remember once again that this "male testing" is *not necessarily conscious* on the part of the female. We have evolved to be this way: Genes that favored this testing tendency in females got passed down successfully over genes that did not. The result is that it *just feels right* to get a certain degree of certainty about a man's intentions before mating.

Cheating

I don't want to give the impression that I could describe the sex roles of men and women accurately and completely even if I devoted the whole book to it. The general roles of he-man, husband/father, and suitor tester describe some of the basic ways men and women behave with each other. But in evolution, anything goes! In fact, we should expect certain individuals to evolve to exploit, manipulate, lie, cheat, and steal in their genes' unstoppable quest to reproduce themselves.

One class of such manipulation is surreptitious mating. For males, this often takes the form of extramarital sex. Interestingly enough, there's not much genetic reason for females to get upset about this other than the possibility that the man will fall in love with the other woman and leave the wife and family.*

For females, the cheating might have involved being secretly impregnated by a he-man with better genes, while not letting the househusband find out. This is not nearly as big a win for the woman's genes as a man's cheating, since it only involves the potential slight improvement of the child's survival against the

---

*David Buss discusses several studies in his book *The Evolution of Desire* (Basic Books, 1994) that show strikingly different causes for jealousy in men and women. In one study performed by Buss himself, 60 percent of men said they would rather their mate develop a deep emotional attachment to another man than have extramarital sex. In contrast, 83 percent of the women said they would prefer sexual infidelity to emotional.

risk that the husband will leave, so we shouldn't expect the drive to be nearly as strong. The unfortunate conclusion is that the pay-off, and hence the drive, is much greater for men cheating with other women. For them, every additional pregnancy is another potential gene-carrying child at virtually no cost to the father.

Time-out Again: Evolutionary "Motives"

Time-out, time-out, time-out! Back up! People having affairs usually *don't want* pregnancies, do they? How can I say that the whole point of cheating is to have more babies when we know people don't want to have babies as a result of affairs?

Once again, the trick is to remember that there's a difference between our conscious thoughts today and the forces of natural selection on DNA in prehistoric times. The *unconscious* tendency to have affairs in certain circumstances is hardwired into people's minds as a result of evolution—as a result of the fact that our ancestors with those tendencies mated to have *us!* Regardless of today's morals, values, or thoughts, we're still stuck with that prehistoric programming that works by making us attracted to, infatuated with, fall in love with, certain other people. We have incredibly strong sex drives as the result of natural selection.

Once we evolved to have those strong sex drives, new klugy uses were able to evolve on top of them. For instance, anthropological studies suggest that one main goal of female infidelity is not getting pregnant but getting other favors—such as more meat for her kids—from the he-man. Conversely, this is why the he-man goes out hunting. Not because it's an efficient way to get protein (it isn't—gathering is much more reliable), but because a big score lets him trade meat for sex all over the village.

And then, of course, there's nothing to stop people from engaging in purely recreational sexual activity in their leisure time. Since natural selection evolved sex-for-reproduction to be so pleasurable, it makes sense that sex-for-its-own-sake, if just a little less pleasurable, would still be a favorite activity as long as it didn't interfere with survival or reproduction.

The Evolution of Cheating

As the tactics and countertactics of mating strategies evolved, cheaters became better and better at cheating and mates became better and better at detecting or preventing it. But the genetic payoff is so large that cheating remains a big factor in the way genes are passed down.

Faking a role is another way of increasing one's chances of genetic payoff. It's tough to fake a he-man role when there are more-dominant men around, because they will tend to put you back in your place quickly, but we could expect a man who quickly notices he's the most dominant male around and "gets tough" to win genetically.

Faking the husband/father role offers much more chance for creativity. The most common ruse for a husband is pretending he's not already married in order to acquire another mating opportunity. For a bachelor, the classic scam is promising eternal love and commitment but leaving after a few romps in the hay. Of course, the women who evolve to be suspicious and discover such behavior have an advantage, so once again we can expect the strategies of cheaters and detectives to have improved over the eons.

This is why bird mating dances are often so long and drawn out, taxing both parties literally to exhaustion. The female bird "knows" (in the evolutionary sense) that no married male will go to that extreme for a one-night stand, at the risk of his real family elsewhere, so she makes him prove he's really single by demanding every ounce of energy he's got to give.

Finding a Niche

If everyone had exactly the same mating strategy, the less-attractive people would always lose out—they would never mate. So some suitors evolved *niche* strategies that might attract fewer potential mates, but mates whom there was less competition for. They got a larger market share of a smaller market, but overall the niche strategy made it more likely for their DNA to be passed on.

Niche mating strategies are why we have different strokes for different folks. While the bulk of men pursue women under 30, who genetically have the most childbearing value, some men prefer older women. While most people are attracted to those with similar facial features, indicating similar DNA, some pursue exotic-looking mates. While most females test suitors before having sex with them, some are extremely promiscuous, perhaps resulting in the offspring getting at least some resources from a slew of potential fathers. Niche mating strategies are a shotgun approach, and the goal is to scatter the DNA as widely as possible.

Mores and Hypocrisy

One way for DNA to increase its chances of winning in the human-reproduction game, aside from doing everything possible to get its own host to reproduce, is to make it more difficult for others to reproduce. In the pre-meme days, powerful males could physically intimidate other males and keep many females for themselves. Males lower on the dominance ladder would be most likely to pass on their DNA by pretending to respect the sanctity of the dominant males' harem but secretly taking advantage of whatever mating opportunities they could find. Studies show chimpanzees engaging in just this behavior.

When memes arrived on the scene, it became in the genetic interest of males to spread memes that would decrease the likelihood of other males' mating. It was in the interest of females' DNA to spread memes promoting good behavior in their suitors. It was in the interest of grandparents to spread memes that would result in the successful rearing of their grandchildren. Thus were born the concepts of *sexual mores*.

Sexual mores are rules of the game, so to speak. They are strategy-memes saying *Don't do this thing you have a desire for.* They keep you from mating with some class of potential mate. People get programmed with them as they are being raised.

> The interesting thing about sexual mores is that when you get programmed with one, you may actually be behaving counter to the interest of your selfish DNA.

It's easy to tell what your DNA wants: just notice who you're sexually attracted to. That's a good indication that, genetically, mating with that person would be useful in passing down your DNA.

Some of the first known sexual prohibitions—those in the Ten Commandments—fit right into this model. Two of the commandments forbid a man having sex with, or even coveting, another man's wife. Men who put that big investment into a home and family only to become cuckolded—referring to the cuckoo bird, which manipulates other birds into raising its young—lose big in the evolutionary game, and so might be expected to spread memes discouraging other men from having affairs with their wives.

But following sexual mores makes you behave in the interest of *everyone else's* DNA, not your own. So the optimal selfish-gene strategy, before people became conscious and had the possibility of a life about something other than spreading their DNA, was to participate in spreading mores but to secretly ignore them whenever an opportunity arose to mate counter to them. That is the evolutionary explanation for hypocrisy. We should expect to see the most hypocrisy around sex, since it's simultaneously in everyone's DNA's advantage both to spread antisex memes and to selfishly ignore them.

From Different Planets

Although sometimes it seems like men and women are from different planets, given how we often have trouble comprehending each other, the basic differences all come from this battle of the sexes I've just talked about. Men, generally, tend to be interested in power, in their place in the hierarchy, in seizing opportunities for sex as quickly and effectively as possible. Generally, they are

Evolutionary psychology can help explain why people are hypocritical about sex. While spreading memes that decrease others' promiscuity, such as *Adultery is wrong,* the hypocrite takes advantage of the very mating opportunities he speaks against. The DNA of people who do that spreads faster than the DNA of honest folk.

most attracted to women who have the most reproductive potential—who are young and healthy. Typically, they are possessive of their women, guarding against being cuckolded.

Women, generally, tend to value security, commitment, and men who are willing to invest in them. As a rule, they are most attracted to two types of men: the strong and powerful, and the committed and generous. Generally, they guard against their man being stolen away by another woman and are on the lookout for any evidence that a man may be losing interest and do anything possible to correct the situation.

Ever wonder why men tend to sneak peeks at attractive women? It was evolutionarily important for them to size up and react to mating opportunities quickly. For the same reason, men get quickly aroused by visual stimuli, which is why today pornography is much more popular with men than with women.

> Men naturally try to impress women with their strength and power. And it works.

Ever wonder why a woman gets upset if a man doesn't call her for a week? To her, it endangers the safety and security of the day-to-day relationship that she has been genetically bred to crave, and her defense mechanisms kick into action. Even if she is mature and confident, she's still likely to feel upset—it's a powerful, primal feeling.

> Women naturally test men to make sure they're really committed and not just faking it. And it works.

Over the last few centuries, these sex roles have been affected greatly by meme evolution, so we find men and women being less successful at reproducing, more frustrated in their relationships, and all around more confused as the primitive societies we evolved to live in have been supplanted by incredibly complicated and powerful cultural forces. But these drives we have been bred with are still with us, and mind viruses take advantage of them; they hook us.

Different cultures today have evolved different sets of sexual mores, resulting in differences in male and female behavior. In Sweden, a social democracy where women have great economic independence, we see a high degree of sexual freedom among women. Without needing to depend on men for their security, Swedish women need not be concerned so much with testing potential mates for commitment and generosity. The result is greater promiscuity among women: a study showed Swedish men prize a potential mate's virginity very little compared with other cultures. Swedish men, in turn, are among the least violent of any culture: with women more available, men need not engage in the violent, risky he-man behavior that comes from a genetic drive to rise in the hierarchy and therefore have greater access to women. Harsh punishment for violent crime isn't necessary.

In sexually strict Saudi Arabia, we see the opposite. Women are highly dependent on men for economic security. Access to sex is greatly restricted for Saudi women. Men prize virginity in their potential mates. Violence is high—an artifact of prehistoric times when engaging in such behavior increased a man's chances of mating—and punishment for violent crime is severe in reaction to that.

> Access to sex is the driving force behind many aspects of culture.

Through a chain of cause and effect, the availability of females for men to mate with can shape prevailing mores, the amount of violence, and the laws and punishments of a culture. There has been a shift in sexual mores in the United States from the free-love era of the '60s, when a baby-boom surplus of young women "did their own thing" sexually, to the AIDS-fearful '90s, when young women were admonished to "just say no" and abstain from sex. This shift has been accompanied by an increase in violent crime among men, as would be predicted by this model.

Sex Buttons

Let's recap the buttons we have that stem from the mating drive and its associated roles. The first three are primarily male buttons, and the second three primarily female; however, the klugy nature of evolution and the importance of niche mating strategies seem to scramble these on occasion, and it's not uncommon to see men with "female" buttons and women with "male" ones. After all, we're members of the same species!

— **Power.** Men pay special attention to opportunities for power. This includes controlling territory, be it physical land or a conceptual landscape such as the software market or the U.S. Senate. In prehistoric times, this would make them more attractive to women. While prehistoric women might seek power to enhance their survival ability, their attractiveness was primarily based on youth and health—their reproductive potential—so they had less selection pressure to develop a *power* button.

— **Dominance.** Men are concerned with their place in the dominance hierarchy. Prehistorically, a higher place in the hierarchy would give access to women without the necessity of a physical fight, costly to the survival of both suitors. Women had less need for this drive, as they were the ones doing the picking and choosing.

— **Window of opportunity.** Men had little to lose and much to gain, DNA-wise, by seizing mating opportunities as often as possible. This ability to recognize a window of opportunity carries over into other areas. ("If you order before midnight tonight, you'll also get a free Ginsu knife!") For women, since having a child is a nine-month investment, they instead evolved patience.

— **Security.** Women look for security. Prehistorically, this drive added to the likelihood of their children surviving to reproduce. It's interesting that virtually all of the U.S. government programs having to do with financing people's security were passed in the relatively brief time since women have had the right to vote. While men value security, they are much more likely to take risks that will increase their status in the hierarchy.

— **Commitment.** Women are attracted to men who display commitment—who show up repeatedly over a period of time. This button gets pushed by advertisers mercilessly to create brand loyalty. Men evolved to be interested in mating with a variety of women.

— **Investment.** Women pay attention to men who invest in them. That's what keeps the flower industry going. Men can pretty much depend on the universal female tendency to nurture the young, and so didn't evolve to look for this in women.

Sexual reproduction is the number one force behind genetic evolution. We evolved instincts and tendencies that supported maximum success in mating back before our culture started evolving. Now here we are in the 21st century, and still hardwired for caveman days. No wonder the self-help section in the bookstore is overflowing with titles!

The Future of Sex

All these instincts and drives evolved to increase the likelihood of women getting pregnant and having babies. But as I mentioned earlier, our conscious thoughts are often oriented in the other direction! Men just want to have sex, right? They don't want the women to get pregnant. Under this model, why do people use birth control? Why do men get vasectomies? It's *not* to support our DNA!

The answer is:

> The millions of years of genetic evolution that produced these instincts did not count on our figuring out that we could have sex and not get pregnant.

We've thrown a huge monkey wrench—or perhaps a rubber sheath would be a better figure of speech—into the genetic works. We've figured out how to have sex without having babies, and as a result, the act of mating is no longer the genetic prize it was for millions of years. Our instincts still think mating equals reproduction, and that's why our sex drives are still so strong.

But now everything has changed. What really benefits our selfish DNA now is the *baby-making* drive: choosing to have a baby. In future generations, through genetic evolution, choosing to have babies will become more and more compelling. If we were *really* responsible about use of birth control and never having unplanned pregnancies, the now-useless sex drive would even atrophy!

I wouldn't count on it, though. Natural selection works quickly to punish lack of reproduction. With governments now guaranteeing the health and well-being of all children, we should expect that segment of the population to grow who don't use birth control. That includes people who think they have good genes and want to reproduce them, but it also includes the irresponsible and the uneducated. And some religions forbid birth control: a genetically winning strategy!

> Like it or not, we only live a few years, and the DNA of those of us who have a tendency not to have children will soon die out. Those of us who have only a few children will be swamped by those who have many.

So if we were living unconsciously, our drives would direct our behavior to maximize our DNA's chances of spreading. Living with the programming of society's mores, we don't even get that. What about those of us who don't have children? What about homosexuals? How can homosexuality survive natural selection? That's one of the toughest questions evolutionary biologists have had to face in applying Darwinism to human beings.

One theory is simply that evolution is in a state of flux right now. As memes have recently become more important than genes, our DNA hasn't yet caught up. If this is the case, it will certainly catch up soon, and we'd expect to see higher birthrates over most of the population.

Another possibility is that those of us who don't have children have become in effect genetic slaves of those of us who do. The child bearers have spread the right combination of memes, infected us with the right viruses of the mind, to keep us happily working to make the world a better place for *their* children. That's one possibility if we look at life from the point of view of spreading DNA.

But life doesn't have to be about spreading DNA at all.

> All these buttons and tendencies can be recognized and overcome. Life can be about something bigger. But unless we understand how we're wired, we can't begin to program ourselves for whatever purpose we want for our lives.

The complex and varied evolution of our sex drive gives us many of the most powerful buttons and tendencies that mind viruses use to program us. The number two drive, right behind sex, is survival. That's where we'll look for the next set of buttons that viruses of the mind exploit.

CHAPTER SEVEN

SURVIVAL AND FEAR

"We will now discuss in a little
more detail the struggle for existence."

— Charles Darwin

In prehistoric times, the most effective way to stay alive was to have a good, healthy relationship with two things: food and danger. The part of our brains that evolved to be attentive to danger was a huge help in the days when we had lots of threats to our survival in everyday life. I wonder how long it was, though, after the invention of language that the first con artist separated the first sucker from his savings by making up a lie about some danger: "Hey, Og! Me saw saber-toothed tiger go in cave where you left food! Better stay away! Heh-heh."

Many myths and religions have some kind of threat of retribution from their god or gods, and their doctrines warn of the dangers of doing various forbidden things. Why? Because memes involving danger are the ones we pay attention to! As oral traditions developed, our brains were set up to amplify the dangers and give them greater significance than the rest.

Once again, meme evolution took off the instant that communication of danger started taking place. Today, having eliminated most day-to-day threats to our survival, we find that our lives are still filled with *danger* memes. The more dangerous, the more we pay attention to them. Just look at all the attention we pay to, and the size of the industries built around, horror films and insurance against loss. There are safety films, of course, but who wants to go see *them?* The most effective "safety film" in my high-school driver's-ed course was called *Mechanized Death.* In contrast to all the boring films outlining normal, safe driving habits, *Mechanized Death* showed several gory accident scenes, graphically depicting the danger inherent in driving unsafely. Although it was only one class period out of 25 or so, it's the one I remember, probably because danger was the only thing powerful enough to distract my attention from its normal high-school priorities: lunch and girls. Danger, food, and sex.

The Evolution of Fear

Because evolution favored safety, we have a lot more fear than we need. *Why* did evolution favor safety? Simple: safety was a prime factor in reproduction. If we stayed safe, we lived to possibly reproduce; if not, we didn't. Genetic evolution wasn't interested in the quality of our lives, only the quantity of our offspring. Naturally—and I literally mean *naturally,* through the course of natural selection—staying safe became a more and more important drive in us and other animals. As with our other drives, it has a feeling associated with it: fear.*

---

*There is another drive associated with safety, too, that I might call *revulsion.* In another example of the klugy nature of evolution, and for no particular reason, we feel revolted by certain dangers and afraid of others. I would guess that revulsion is an older, simpler mechanism than fear. I say that because the things we tend to be revolted by are very old dangers such as visibly diseased bodies, noxious fumes, and poisonous tastes. Nature has separately evolved many safety-oriented drives: even the most primitive single-celled organisms tend to move away from hostile environments and toward more fruitful ones.

Fear is highly adaptive to whatever the current situation is. The fact that one person might be scared witless to walk down the same dark street that inspired Gene Kelly to sing in the rain shows that specific fears are far from universal among human beings. In fact, since I used to be petrified of public speaking and now I look forward to it, I can say with confidence that fears change even within a single person's lifetime.

> Human fear is generated by "hardware" instincts viewing life through memetic "software" programming. That programming consists of all the distinction-memes, strategy-memes, and association-memes you got from everything you've ever experienced, heard, thought, or been taught.

It's an incredible genetic leap that allowed us, and whatever other animals possess the ability, to protect ourselves against dangers we learn about only after we are born and our genes are fixed.

Imagine the genetic process that resulted in the evolution of fear: Let's say there are some prehistoric animals, Spot and Rover, who have figured out how to communicate the concept of *danger*. Spot has seen a tiger in a cave over yonder. He says to Rover, as he runs like the dickens in the other direction, "Rover—*pant, pant*—old fellow, there's danger in the—*pant, pant*—cave over yonder." Rover then acts just like he would have if he had *seen* a tiger, and runs like the dickens. This makes him less likely to be eaten and is generally a favorable evolutionary adaptation. By the way, simply noticing Spot running like that might have been the only communication necessary.

But all that running is a bit of a waste of energy, which is going to wear Spot out and make him hungry, which will require food. Poor Spot probably does better than his predecessors, who had no ability to even become aware of the danger, but there's still room for improvement.

So Spot's mate has a litter or six, and one of those offspring—Spot, Jr.—has a slightly different reaction: heightened awareness of danger, but not actually running until there's a better reason. Since he achieves the same benefit as Spot without the cost of tuckering himself out and therefore making himself hungry, thirsty, and more vulnerable to attack, the genes responsible for the Spot, Jrs., of the world, over time, will displace the genes of Spot.

Time passed, genes evolved, and we found ourselves with several very identifiable feelings all having to do with danger. That heightened awareness of some nonspecific danger is called *anxiety*. Good old *fear* is associated with a danger that we have the instinct to run away from. If instead our reaction is to stick around and fight, we feel *anger*. Then we've got mixtures and shades of these feelings, all with their own names: nervousness, worry, suspicion, trepidation, and so on. Just as the Eskimos have lots of words for *snow*, the richness of our *danger* vocabulary illustrates the evolutionary fact that the concept is a central one to our lives. As if we needed proof.

What Went Wrong?

Why has fear—this wonderful, complex, adaptive response to danger—become such a burden on our modern lives? Why are so many people in therapy, so many *more* reading self-improvement books, and, sadly, so many *more still* quietly despairing, all because their lives are filled with unwanted fear? Why did our responses to danger, which served us well for so long during our genetic evolution, suddenly turn against us and become the main roadblock in realizing our full potential in life?

It's a complicated subject, perhaps rivaling sex in its ubiquitous intertwining in the fabric of our lives. The common thread, though, is this: we now live in an environment so far removed from the millennia during which our genes evolved that the fear/anger/danger mechanism is no longer appropriate to the task.

Our lives today are about jobs, societies, and ideas—not lions, tigers, and bears. But people treat cultural failure as if it were as harmful as physical failure—being eaten! The instinctive reactions and emotions that evolution equipped us with are frankly bad for anyone who is interested in more than survival. It is an area where the New Age truism "Trust your instincts" fails us.

> Success in life depends upon perseverance in the face of failure, yet our instincts about cultural dangers send us in just the opposite direction.

Today's environment is largely the invention of our minds. Our fear sensors have gone haywire! Imagine that the part of our minds that produces fear is like a supermarket bar-code reader installed in our heads. When it sees something it recognizes as scary, it beeps and rings up a price—how scared we get by any situation. A million years ago, the scanners worked great: everything we looked at had nice neat UPC codes printed on it. But the situations the scanners were built to recognize no longer exist—now we're aiming our bar-code readers at striped neckties, Jackson Pollock paintings, and psychedelic light shows. It's a wonder we get along as well as we do!

Actually, we don't get along that well. We live in an age of great confusion and stress. Anyone who's ever had the desire to "get away from it all" has felt the pull of a simpler, less confusing environment: one that our senses were designed to make sense of.

Fear and Kinship

We don't just pay special attention to our own dangers. Since our genes are shared by our relatives, we also find our attention attracted to situations where we might help people sharing our genes at little cost to ourselves. We call this *altruism,* and interestingly society seems to smile as surely on altruism as it frowns on personal indulgence. Both, however, evolved from the fittest genes' survival. Here are some button-pushing memes relating to altruism:

— **Helping children.** The best thing you can do for your selfish genes, next to surviving and reproducing, is helping your children or other children who share those genes survive to reproduce themselves. Scientists aren't through by any means with their investigation of behavior toward children in humans, which runs the gamut from helping children of other races to killing one's own children. As a general rule, though, many people have an instinct for *helping children.*

— **Birds of a feather.** Groups of people with like genes who hang out together and help each other have a better chance of survival, and also of keeping their gene pool from being diluted by outsiders.

At last! Some nice memes! We're not just base, vile creatures after all, are we? But the fact that genes evolved to care more about themselves than individual people has a nasty side, too. How about these memes:

— **Racism.** Excluding or even fighting people with obviously different genes, the seamy side of *birds of a feather,* has the effect of preserving the status quo of the gene pool. This is currently frowned upon by mainstream American society, although until the 20th century it was well accepted in most cultures that had exposure to other races.

— **Elitism.** Any group of people who share and act on the belief that they deserve better resources, privileges, or treatment than others are more likely to survive and propagate their genes in times of scarcity.

Helping children, birds of a feather, racism, and *elitism* are all memes that push our buttons. Along with *crisis, danger,* and some more complicated fear-based memes I'll discuss later in the chapter, these button-pushing memes are prime candidates for mind viruses to take advantage of in attracting our attention and penetrating our defenses. And the danger doesn't have to be real—we just have to think it might be.

To get along in the modern world, we need to ignore our senses to a degree and live by the ideas, customs, and beliefs that exist solely in our minds. The fear reaction, though, seems to be one of the most difficult instincts to ignore. For that reason, memes that invoke a fear reaction, and the attention we pay along with it, have done very well indeed. Here are some of the ways memes have evolved to take advantage of our fear buttons.

Save the Children!
before it's too late . . .

Children all over the world are in danger! Without a first-hand understanding of memetics, they are prone to infection by *mind viruses*—infections that could *literally destroy* the quality of their lives.

What can you do to help? Teach them memetics. But time is short. Your help is needed *now.* If you know any children in high school or college, don't wait for someone else to help them. Be the one friend they can count on. Make a difference in their lives and the lives of the next generation. Invest in their future now. Give them a copy of *Virus of the Mind* today.

By framing something as a cultural "danger," advertisers can make people at least pay attention to their ads. Viruses of the mind often include fear-inducing memes.

The Psychology of Gambling

When I was just beginning to get interested in how the mind works, one of the topics most fascinating to me was the psychology of gambling. Why do people gamble against the house, knowing full well that the house has the advantage? More to the point, how could I make money by taking advantage of the fact that other people sometimes made bad bets?

The secret is that gamblers' instincts stem from prehistoric times and give them bad advice in a world deliberately designed to fool them. Some of those false instincts are:

117

— **Overvaluing a long shot.** In prehistoric times, engaging in a low-risk, high-reward activity such as searching for food was of survival benefit, even if the reward appeared only occasionally. In gambling games with huge payoffs such as lotto and keno, the true odds can be absolutely abysmal. People will still play because of the low risk and high reward.

— **Cheap insurance.** Another low-risk, high-reward meme is "cheap insurance." That means putting forth some small effort in order to reduce the risk of danger, like camouflaging your cave entrance before going to sleep. In my blackjack-playing years, many times I heard the common wisdom that you should always "buy insurance"—make an additional bet that the dealer has blackjack—when you have blackjack yourself. Analysis of the game shows that insurance is a bad bet, blackjack or no; but the *cheap insurance* meme makes it intuitively appealing.

— **Playing the streaks.** In life, despite the disclaimers of certain mutual-fund advertisements, past performance is usually a pretty good indicator of future results. If deer have been gathering at the watering hole every day at dawn for the last week, chances are that they will again tomorrow. In most games of chance, though, each play is completely independent of the past. Streaks are just random events, yet people gamble as if they had some significance.

— **Playing against the streaks.** In a wonderful example of the basic inconsistency of the human race, some people have developed the instinct to go against the flow, contrary to mass opinion. It's easy to see how this might have survival advantages in finding food or mates, since it automatically lessens one's competition; however, in gambling on random events, it's just as useless a strategy as going *with* the flow or streak.

— **Being stingy when you're down, generous when you're up.** The survival instinct to conserve scarce resources and be more lavish when resources are abundant is the exact opposite of the optimal money-management strategy. Computer modeling shows that you will last the longest before going broke if you bet more when you're behind, less when you're ahead.

— **Playing a hunch.** Occasionally trying a new strategy or a creative approach was and is useful for survival. It's not useful for most gambling games, though, especially blackjack: there's exactly one way to play each hand that will result in the best odds of winning. Casinos make millions on blackjack players' hunches that deviate from that somewhat boring strategy.

It's not just that people gamble poorly because of these false instincts: gambling games have *evolved* to exploit these tendencies! The casinos made money on the games that best fooled us, such as blackjack, and replicated them. Over time, weaker games such as faro faded out, not bringing in as large a profit to the house.

Expected Payoffs on a $10 Bet When Player Has Blackjack					
Amount of bet	Payoff if dealer has blackjack	Payoff if dealer does not have blackjack	Odds dealer has blackjack	Odds dealer does not have blackjack	Total expected payoff
$10 + $5 insurance	$20	$20	15/49 = 0.31	34/49 = 0.69	$20.00
$10, no insurance	$10	$25	15/49 = 0.31	34/49 = 0.69	$20.41

Insuring blackjack is a bad bet unless you've been counting cards and know there are unusually many tens left in the deck. But the *cheap insurance* meme tempts people to make the bet anyway.

Memes that exploit these tendencies have found their way into other parts of our culture, too. Being conscious of these tendencies could not only improve your success as a gambler, but also enhance the quality of other areas of your life.

Urban Legends

It's tempting to think that myths, proverbs, legends, and oral traditions are passed down because of either their factual truth or their particular usefulness in our lives—lessons, perhaps, or the wisdom of the ages. Being experts on memes, though, we now know that the stories, myths, and common wisdom that survive are the ones with—you guessed it—good memes.

Let's take a look at some of our modern urban legends, those stories that won't die no matter how many times they're refuted. Why won't they die? Because a boring newspaper story saying "nothing interesting or dangerous is actually happening at all" cannot hope to compete with a scary urban legend full of juicy memes! Here are some of my favorites, with the buttons pushed by the memes inserted in brackets:

A boy is dying of leukemia *[crisis]*. Before he dies, he wants to see if he can make it into the *Guinness Book of World Records [mission]* by setting the record for collecting the most get-well cards *[distinguishing yourself]*. Please help him *[helping children]* by sending him a card *[low risk, high reward]*.

A couple goes to a garage sale and argues over whether to buy a beat-up chair for $5 *[opportunity]*. They decide to buy the chair. When they get it home, the dog starts sniffing and scratching at the upholstery *[danger]*. They examine the torn corner of the seat cover and discover a plain brown bag with $38,000 in $100 bills in it *[low risk, high reward]*.

Soap giant Procter & Gamble has been receiving complaint letters for decades from people who have heard that their century-old man-in-the-moon logo is actually a satanic symbol *[danger]* and want them to change it in the name of God *[mission]*.

Somebody found a (your favorite nasty substance) *[danger]* in their (your favorite food item) *[food]* at (your favorite fast-food restaurant) *[familiarity]*. They sued them and got $2 million *[low risk, high reward]*.

Superstition

Are you superstitious? Even if you're not, you probably can name more things that supposedly bring good or bad luck than you can name Presidents of the United States. Assuming for the moment that there is no real-world validity to these claims (knock on wood), why do we all know so many superstitions?

Hint: this will have something to do with fear and memes.

Most superstitions are based on the *cheap insurance* meme. For the apparently low cost of avoiding black cats, staying home on Friday the 13th, or tossing a bit of salt over your left shoulder— and it must be the *left* shoulder—you get cheap insurance against something bad happening.

Some superstitions throw in other memes, especially *playing the streaks*. Craps players want a successful shooter (the one who rolls the dice) to continue rolling until his winning streak ends. They get more and more excited with each random victory. Athletes commonly don't change their underwear during a winning streak. Baseball player Wade Boggs ate chicken before every game. He says he didn't eat it once and went hitless with three errors at third base. Can you blame him?

My friend Greg Kusnick, whom you'll remember from the conversation in the Microsoft cafeteria where I first heard about memes, has a habit of getting up each morning and glancing at the newspaper headlines on his way out the door. Just a glance, that's all. One day he didn't do it, and the Pope died. Of course, the Pope had already died long before Kusnick failed to look at the newspaper, but rational thought has little to do with superstition! As Kusnick recalls:

I couldn't escape the spooky feeling that it was somehow my fault. I failed in my duty . . . and when the dust settled, the Pope was dead.

Are superstitions bad? Only in the sense that if you are paying attention to salt and cats, you may miss out on something you would find more worthwhile. Or if you think your bad luck is being caused by that mirror you broke last year, you might not search hard enough for some real causes that you might be able to do something about. Maybe you have bad breath!

How do superstitions get started? All different ways. People make them up as a joke or prank, someone notices a seeming pattern in chance events—the initial origin doesn't matter so much as why they get perpetuated.

> Superstitions get perpetuated because they have what it takes from a meme's point of view: the *cheap insurance* component of superstitions just presses our button.

We pay attention to them. And since there are few things we love to talk about more than danger, we pass these superstitions around freely. So superstitions become viruses of the mind, diverting our attention, affecting our behavior, and programming us to spread them to others.

I ran into perhaps the origin of a new superstition on my national tour to promote my first book, *Getting Past OK*. In three separate cities, I heard a rumor going around that youth gangs had a new rite of initiation. A group of them would ride around after dark in a car with its headlights turned off. The first Good Samaritan to flash his or her lights as a friendly reminder would be hunted down and killed.

Danger! Crisis! And, of course, cheap insurance: just don't flash your lights and you're safe. The story seems to have been a hoax, the result of a series of planted fax messages to radio and TV stations around the country, but it has every element of a good urban legend or superstition. I would not be surprised, 50 years from now, to see people avoiding flashing their headlights much as they avoid stepping on a crack in the sidewalk, with only the vaguest notion of the origins of the superstition.

The genetic tendency we have to pass the word about dangerous situations served us well a long time ago. But once that mechanism was established, it opened the gates for individual superstitions to have a field day inhabiting some choice real estate in our minds.

There is one big danger in living life with this outdated reverence we have for fear and its associated memes: making bad decisions based on fear. Because our instinctive reaction is to give this emotion much more weight than it deserves in modern life, we often miss out on great opportunities.

Getting Past Fear

Our tendency to overreact to cultural "dangers" applies not only to superstitions but to many things we fear in everyday life: people's disapproval, failing to meet a goal, rejection, and so on. It all boils down to the fact that our fear-reaction mechanisms are still calibrated for a time when the world was full of real threats to our survival and reproduction.

> There used to be lots of good reasons to be afraid. Now there aren't.

Overcoming fear requires you to train yourself to think every time you feel fear, rather than just reacting instinctively. The thought process I go through goes like this:

I'm scared. Is it physical danger? No. Well, when I make a decision based on fear, it's often a bad one, so I'm going to put the fear aside and ask myself, "What is my purpose in this situation?" I'll make my decision consciously based on what

*helps achieve my purpose better, rather than unconsciously on
my instinctive desire to run away from fear.*

Sound kind of awkward and nerdy? That logical thought process was essential to my overcoming my stage fright and becoming a public speaker. After a while, it became second nature and I
didn't need to think all the words anymore; I just seemed to have
created a new unconscious thought pattern—a strategy-meme—
that supported my agenda rather than some prehistoric DNA's.
Logic is a wonderful thing. A boring truth seldom taught in success seminars is that clear, logical thinking and simply plodding
ahead with a plan are great tools for success in life.

Genetic evolution gave us the *tendency* to pay attention to certain memes. Note that I said "tendency," not "mandate." We have
the ability to consciously override our genetic programming and
even over time to reprogram ourselves to unconsciously pay attention to other things, if we decide other things are more important.

So if the effect on you of your animal heritage ended there, it
wouldn't be too bad. You could go through life, chuckling every
once in a while as you noticed your attention being diverted in
one of these genetic directions. You'd at least be secure in the
knowledge that even though you were siphoning off some of your
consciousness, you were contributing to evolution. This assumes
you care to have some purpose to your life other than just surviving. If you just want to survive, you're in great shape—you will
indeed survive until you die—and you can stop reading now. Natural selection will select your genes or not, as it wishes. By the way,
if you do choose to devote your life to the service of your genes, I'll
give you a hint: they want you to have as many kids as possible.

For the rest of us, though, it doesn't end there. Remember,
we've still got these viruses of the mind to deal with. And now that
we know what the buttons are that memes can push, let's take a
look at how we get programmed.

CHAPTER EIGHT

HOW WE GET PROGRAMMED

"There are two kinds of people in this world: those that enter a room and turn the television set on, and those that enter a room and turn the television set off."

— Raymond Shaw, the protagonist
in the movie *The Manchurian Candidate*

Here's the chapter you've all been waiting for. It's all about how to manipulate people, using memes and genetic buttons, into doing exactly what you want them to do. Heh-heh.

You know what a meme is—a thought, belief, or attitude in your mind that can spread to and from other people's minds. You know that we human beings are the medium for the evolution of memes. You understand how evolution works by natural selection—survival of the fittest. And you've seen how our own genetic evolution gives us *buttons:* tendencies to pay special attention to certain things—especially danger, food, and sex—which helped us survive and reproduce in prehistoric times.

Now comes the scary, upsetting part.

> Memes enter our minds without our permission. They become part of our mental programming and influence our lives without our even being aware of it.

In this chapter, I'll show how we get programmed by new memes and start to discuss what we can do to prevent being infected by unwanted programming.

Meme Infection

We get infected by new memes in three ways. I'll introduce each of the ways now, then discuss each in more detail later.

— The first way we get infected is through **conditioning**, or repetition. If we hear something repeated often enough, it becomes part of our programming. Advertisers and salespeople know this well. Any good book on sales will tell you that most customers don't buy until they have been asked five to seven times. It takes that many repetitions to implant the *Buy me* meme in the customer.

— The second way is through a mechanism known as **cognitive dissonance**. When things don't make sense, our minds struggles to *make* them make sense.

Imagine, for example, that a friend is upset with you, but you don't know why. You have two memes that conflict—that are inconsistent: *friend* and *upset with me*. You resolve the conflict, or dissonance, by creating new memes, by rearranging your memetic programming so that things make sense again. *Ah, Bill's upset because he's paid for lunch the last three times,* you might conclude. Right or wrong, you now have a new meme about Bill and lunch that will influence your future behavior.

I've heard it said that geniuses develop their most brilliant original thoughts through self-imposed cognitive dissonance. As you might guess, then, as a programming method it is particularly effective with intelligent people, because you actually believe that the new meme is your own idea.

— The third way new memes enter our minds is by taking advantage of our genetic buttons in the manner of the **Trojan horse**. As we have seen, because of our nature there are certain things we tend to pay special attention to, such as warnings of danger, cries of children, and sexual attractiveness. We are susceptible to bundles of memes that push our buttons to get our attention and then sneak in some other memes along with them.

Simply getting programmed by new memes isn't the same as catching a full-blown mind virus, but viruses of the mind take advantage of one or all of these methods to make their initial inroads into our minds. At the end of this chapter, I'll put it all together and show how these various ingredients combine to make viruses of the mind.

Conditioning

Conditioning—programming by repetition—is the easiest way to acquire memes that don't push any of your buttons effectively. For instance, if you want to learn French, you listen to people speaking that language as you study the lexicon. At first it just sounds like people clearing their throats and moaning, but after many repetitions, you begin to be programmed with distinction-memes. Soon you can begin to distinguish French words and sentences where there was meaninglessness before.

Remember elementary school? Learning to read and write? Memorizing the multiplication table? I have two memories from first grade. One is being incredibly bored by doing arithmetic problems over and over and over again. The other is being incredibly frustrated by the teacher's reading of the same page of "See Spot run" over and over and over again. Frustrated or bored, it didn't matter: conditioning by repetition works.

Elementary-school programming by conditioning was not limited to reading, writing, and arithmetic. We pledged allegiance to the flag of the United States of America every morning. Repetition. Conditioning. And there's one thing all native-born Americans know for sure: the United States is one nation, indivisible, with liberty and justice for all. Right?

That patriotism didn't spontaneously arise in each of us out of our spiritual nature: we were programmed! And it wasn't presented to us as a reasoned, logical argument: we just said it and heard it enough times and—poof!—it became one of our beliefs, our values, our memes. Long-term prisoners can become "institutionalized"—they become so conditioned to the culture inside prison that they no longer want to live outside. They try to get back in once they're released. There's no reason to think that the long-term conditioning of a bad job or a bad marriage doesn't have the same effect.

Children typically get programmed with religious beliefs through conditioning by repetition. Whatever the religion, children go from zero beliefs to full-fledged faith, or as "fledged" as they get, by being told about the divinity of God or Jesus or David Koresh over and over again until it becomes real—those memes become programmed.

If you listen repeatedly to religious speech, after enough repetitions you will actually begin to notice God and His works where there was just chaotic life going on before. What was formerly chance becomes a miracle. What was pain is now karma. What was human nature is now sin. And regardless of whether these religious memes are presented as Truth or as allegorical mythology, you're conditioned just the same.

> You can be conditioned, through repetition, to acquire new distinction-memes that make reality look different to you and provide reinforcing evidence that keeps those distinction-memes in place.

In psychology, the word *conditioning* often refers to implanting association-memes. Pavlov's dog was *conditioned* to associate the ringing bell with yummy food. When the Coca-Cola Company pays millions of dollars to show you young people in bathing suits having a good time drinking their products, they are *conditioning* you to associate good feelings with their brands. The repetition of that commercial creates association-memes in your mind so that when you push your shopping cart down the soft-drink aisle, you get an irrational urge to buy Coke. It's possible to override that urge through conscious intention or the fact that other memes are stronger, but the urge makes a difference in their bottom line* or they wouldn't be spending the money.

There's also a term for the use of repetition to create strategy-memes: *operant conditioning.* Viewing commercials or listening to bells ring is passive; it involves no activity or strategy. When you behave in some way and that behavior gets rewarded, that is operant conditioning. The reward creates and reinforces strategy-memes.

The classic example of operant conditioning is teaching a rat to run a maze. At first, the rat just wanders around. But soon he discovers there is a yummy piece of cheese tucked away in one cor-ner—a reward. Quickly, the rat learns to run directly to the cheese rather than just wandering.

We use operant conditioning on our children constantly: grad-ing their schoolwork, praising them when they do things we like. The repetition of these rewards conditions the children to behave in a certain way. It creates and reinforces strategy-memes that, if we are good parents and teachers, will serve them as adults in their pursuit of happiness.

However, operant conditioning can be used for many other purposes besides training you to pursue happiness. Whenever you're in a repeated situation in which a reward is available for certain behavior, you are being conditioned.

---

*At least they *think* it makes a difference. They may be fooled by their own memetic programming! More on this in Chapter 9.

> If you're in a situation where you're being rewarded for some behavior, think about what memes that operant conditioning is programming you with. Do they serve your purpose in life?

Cognitive Dissonance

Another programming technique is creating mental pressure and resolving it—*cognitive dissonance*. Why do high-pressure sales tactics exist even though people universally despise them? As with any "why" question in the world of memetics, the answer is: *because the meme for it is good at spreading*. Salespeople get infected with the *high-pressure sales* meme and go about acting on it, regardless of whether it's the most effective means at their disposal. There's no question, however, that it does work on some people some of the time.

High-pressure sales work by making you mentally uncomfortable—by creating cognitive dissonance. You enter the situation with some strategy-memes that make you resist buying: perhaps they are something like *Look before you leap* or *Shop around before you buy*. The salesperson programs you with a meme making it attractive to buy immediately: *If I don't buy now, I'll miss a window of opportunity* or even simply *If I buy now, the salesperson will like me*.

> Those new memes conflict with your old ones, and a mental tension is created. Your mind wants to resolve the conflict. It does so by creating a new meme.

There are two ways to release the pressure caused by cognitive dissonance: buy in or bail out. If you bail out, it's likely to be because you've resolved the dissonance by creating a meme such as *The salesperson is a jerk*. But some people buy, creating instead a meme like *I really want to buy this*. Once you create that meme, it's yours, and a smart salesperson will reinforce it by telling you what a smart decision you've made and even calling a few days later and congratulating you on your purchase.

Cognitive dissonance can be used to create a meme of submission and loyalty to whatever authority is causing the dissonance. Fraternity hazings, boot camp, and some religious or spiritual disciplines put people through difficult tests and may demand demonstrations of loyalty before releasing the pressure. That creates an association-meme between the demonstration of loyalty and the good feeling caused by the release of pressure.

> With cognitive dissonance, people end up believing they have received something valuable, something deserving of their loyalty, when in reality all that has happened is that the people who were torturing them have stopped.

Prisoners of war have been programmed to submit and be loyal to their captors through this method.

One interesting result of research in operant conditioning on people is that it works better—creates stronger memes—to give the reward only occasionally than it does to give it all the time. That could be because withholding the reward adds cognitive dissonance to the operant conditioning. So a truly manipulative meme programmer will withhold the reward most of the time even if the subject performs flawlessly, knowing this will create stronger programming.

The ramifications of this research are interesting. People often say that the teachers who made the most difference in their education were the tough graders—the ones who withheld the A's much of the time. The occasional A reinforces the *Work hard* meme more than the constant A because it adds cognitive dissonance. Talk shows are filled with people who stay involved in relationships they say are awful most of the time—perhaps the conditioning and dissonance of the occasional reward in a cruddy relationship reinforces the strategy-meme *Stay together* more than it does in a relationship that's good most of the time!

Trojan Horses

The *Trojan horse* method of programming works by getting you to pay attention to one meme, then sneaking in a whole bundle of others along with it. If you're an intelligent, educated person, you may be thinking, *Wow! You must have to be pretty gullible to fall for that!* Tell that to the Trojans.

There are any number of mechanisms for doing the meme bundling. For one, a Trojan horse can take advantage of your instinctive buttons, pushing them to get your attention and then sneaking in another agenda. The simplest example of a button-pushing Trojan horse is the advertising truism "Sex sells." Why does sex sell? Because the sex pushes your button, draws your attention, and acts as a Trojan horse for other memes bundled into the advertisement. Of course, *danger, food, crisis, helping children,* and the other buttons all sell, too, if not quite as well as sex. Much more on this in Chapter 9.

A Trojan horse can also take advantage of the strategy-memes you're currently programmed with having to do with learning or believing. For example, people who have the strategy-meme *If I trust someone, believe what they say* are susceptible to new memetic programming coming from people they trust. People who have the strategy-meme *Believe things consistent with what I know; be skeptical of all else* are susceptible to new memetic programming that *seems* consistent with what they already know. If you're programmed to *believe what X says because it is the voice of God*—where X is a person, a book, or even a practice such as meditation—you're easily programmed with any additional memes that come from X.

The simplest bundling technique, one used frequently by politicians and trial lawyers, is simply saying the memes one after the other, in decreasing order of believability. The credibility of the first statements seem to carry over to the unsupported ones. For example:

We all want freedom!
We all want democracy to work for everyone!

We all want every American to have the opportunity
to pursue the American Dream!
And we all want a national health-care system that
makes that possible.

Now it's a bit of a stretch to conclude that federal management of health care has anything to do with freedom, democracy, or the American Dream, but juxtaposing the statements like that seems to turn off people's natural skepticism.

> The questionable memes at the end of the bundle ride into your mind inside the Trojan horse of the acceptable memes at the beginning.

Bundling the statements together like that is one form of a *Neuro-Linguistic Programming* (NLP) technique known as *embedding,* or packaging memes to make people more susceptible to them.

A related NLP technique is *anchoring:* taking some image, sound, or sensation and linking it to an unrelated idea. For example, a political candidate who gestures at himself when talking about a rosy future and at his opponent when preaching doom and gloom is actually anchoring good feelings to himself and bad feelings to his opponent. The repeated bundling of the gestures with the good and bad feelings creates association-memes in your mind, which will later influence the way you vote.

You can use anchoring on yourself to quickly put yourself in a good or enthusiastic mood! Close your eyes and imagine a time when you were excited and motivated. Create a vivid mental picture. Now, when you are immersed in that motivated feeling, lightly scratch the pad of your index finger with your thumbnail. You're anchoring that state of mind to that sensation.

Open your eyes and come back to the present. Repeat this a few times over a period of days or weeks, and you'll find that next time you want to motivate yourself quickly, a gentle scratch of the pad of your index finger with your thumbnail will get you in the right mood.

As with many of the techniques in this chapter, embedding and anchoring are used a lot by sophisticated salespeople. The whole point of sales is to influence people's beliefs—infect them with certain memes—for direct economic gain. It's natural that we'd see many effective meme-spreading techniques used by salespeople; for that reason, many of the examples in this chapter have to do with selling.

Selling and Programming

An effective form of embedding often used in sales is the question-asking technique. One of the first things you'll learn if you take a good sales-training class is that you must be the one asking the questions. You need to control the interaction by asking the right questions and leading the mark—er—customer down the path leading to the sale. Why is that?

You do it for exactly the same reason a trial lawyer asks a witness very specific questions, rather than just saying, "Uh, anything you want to tell us about the alleged crime?" The attorney has a point she wants to prove and does everything possible to create a framework supporting that point. If you've watched *L.A. Law* or *Perry Mason*, you know there are rules in court prohibiting lawyers from going too far in constructing that framework. A judge wouldn't allow a question like "Did you see the evil defendant, who was thinking to himself, *Hey, that looks like a good house to rob*, skulking in the bushes?"

Why not? That question constructs a tad too much framework. Simply by asking it, the lawyer is creating mental images and attitudes in the minds of the jury. She's using embedding to create memes in someone else's mind without their being aware of it. And that's exactly what the salesperson, not constrained by rules of evidence, is doing to—er—*with* you.

> Asking questions is a Trojan-horse method for infecting people with memes.

Real-estate salespeople are trained to use "you" and "your" as much as possible. "Would *you* like to go up and see *your* master bedroom?" they ask. Simply by posing the question, they create and reinforce an image in your mind of you owning the house. They program you with an association-meme. Pretty sneaky, huh?

Of course, you don't need to ask questions to reinforce these mental images. "Oh, look—here's your fireplace." "You could knock this wall out and have a huge playroom for your kids." "And through this door you've got a garage for both your cars." This is all still embedding. All these help create memes, but wise salespeople know asking questions, especially ones to which your answer is yes, helps get the sale. So another technique is to tag a little question on the end of these statements to program you with the strategy-meme of saying yes:

"This bedroom is gorgeous, isn't it?" "This is just what you were looking for, isn't it?" "I just love this view, don't you?"

> The very act of asking people a question can cause them to create or reinforce a meme in their minds. Asking enough of the right questions can actually change someone's belief system, and therefore influence the person's behavior.

Influencing people's behavior, of course, is exactly the point of sales: you want to influence someone to buy what you're selling. If you're a salesperson, you've probably been using these techniques for years, without always knowing why they work.

Creating Value

The key to effective sales is finding what the customer considers valuable about your product and reinforcing that meme in his mind. Now what the *customer* finds valuable may have nothing whatsoever to do with what the *salesperson* finds valuable. If you're a good salesperson selling a Picasso to someone who likes it because it matches the china, you won't tell him that's not the right reason to like it! You'll sell him another Picasso from his Blue Period because it matches the tablecloth.

The salesperson's job is to create a meme in the customer's mind that says *I believe I'm going to buy this.* The best salespeople don't look upon the sale as an adversarial relationship but as a genuine win-win situation. The customer gets something she wants, and the salesperson gets the commission. So the salesperson will be trying to get you to figure out why you want the product and trying to have you create memes reinforcing your belief in the product's value.

The question-asking technique works well here once again. Someone browsing in a store may easily wander around and leave without buying anything. But if a salesperson comes up and asks, "May I help you find something?" there's a good chance the customer will identify something he's looking for. Simply saying "I'm checking out the lamps" reinforces the idea in the customer's mind that he *wants* a lamp.

Now the salesperson follows up with, "Are you looking for a floor lamp, a table lamp, or a wall fixture?" Whatever the answer, the customer now has a bit clearer picture of what he wants, and his sense of value in actually making a purchase continues to increase.

As the questions become more and more specific, and as the customer gets a clearer picture of what he wants, the likelihood of a sale increases. Now the salesperson can start fishing for other bits of value. "Which room is the lamp for?" "Are you looking to replace a lamp you have there now?" "I've noticed that beautiful women are attracted to men with nice lamps, haven't you?"

Awhile ago, I got a call from a local radio station claiming to be doing a survey. I went along with it, and it went something like this:

> "Do you enjoy listening to music from the '70s, '80s, and '90s?"
> "Sure."
> "Were you aware that KXYZ plays the top hits of the '70s, '80s, and '90s?"

"Uh . . . no, but I guess I am now."

"Since you enjoy listening to the top hits of the '70s, '80s, and '90s, will you be listening to KXYZ more often, the same amount, or less often now?"

"Uh . . . maybe more often."

"Do you usually recommend radio stations to your friends if you enjoy listening to them?"

"Yeah, sometimes. Say, what kind of—"

"Now that you know KXYZ is the best station playing all the top hits of the '70s, '80s, and '90s, are you likely to recommend it to all your friends?"

"Uh . . . maybe . . ."

"Will you in fact take out a full-page ad in the *Seattle Times* proclaiming to the world how wonderful KXYZ is and how everyone in the world should be listening to it all the time?"

"Hey, wait a minute—"

"Have a nice day." Click.

Wow! Pretty great stuff, huh? You're glad you bought this copy of *Virus of the Mind,* aren't you? Reading *Virus of the Mind* could make quite a difference in your quality of life, couldn't it? You're going to rave about *Virus of the Mind* to everyone you meet, aren't you? *Virus of the Mind* would make a great gift, wouldn't it? Heh-heh.

Closing: The Golden Question

Since sales is all about creating memes in customers—that is, programming them in a small way—let's continue to explore sales methods. A salesperson's favorite meme, of course, is, "Yes, I'll take it." Asking a question that results in the creation of that meme is called *closing.* There are all kinds of different and sneaky ways to close. They fall into three camps: *direct, embedded,* and *presumptive.* All have the same goal: to create the *yes* meme in the customer.

The *direct* close includes any straightforward request for the sale, whether tentative or confrontational:

- Are you thinking about buying any copies of *Virus of the Mind* for anyone else in your life?

- Would you be willing to call ten people and warn them of the dangers of mind viruses?

- There are people you know who *need* to read *Virus of the Mind* right now. Go to the bookstore *right now* and buy them each a copy. Okay?

Another way of closing the sale is to use the *embedded* close. The embedded close bypasses the customer's pressure detector by making it seem that the request is not directed at him:

- When you read *Virus of the Mind,* you find you want to tell everybody about it!

- I had one couple come in, and the wife told the husband, "You should buy everyone on your Christmas list a copy of *Virus of the Mind.*"

- I was petting my dog the other day, and I thought, *You should really go into a few of the bookstores in town and make sure they're displaying <u>Virus of the Mind</u> prominently.*

A third way of consummating a sale is to use the *presumptive close*. The presumptive close *presumes* the customer has already made his decision and tricks his mind into creating the *yes* meme:

- Would you like those copies of *Virus of the Mind* sent by Priority Mail or Fourth-Class Book Rate?

- Will that be Visa or MasterCard?

- Is there anyone else you'd like to buy a copy of *Virus of the Mind* for along with yourself?

People use the close to sell things other than products and services. A friend who was a former Mormon missionary told me about a practice they referred to as "GQ-ing people" or "popping the Golden Question." In his case, the Golden Question was, "So, are you willing to accept Jesus as your Savior?" Selling people on a concept—a whole bundle of memes—can have a far greater influence on their lives than selling them even a really great vacuum cleaner.

> When you sell people a bundle of memes, it can program them to spend the rest of their lives behaving the way you want them to.

Marriage is one such memetic bundle commonly entered into by popping a Golden Question. There's no physical reality to a marriage. It's just programming yourself with some new memes. It's adopting distinction-memes for *married couple* and *family*. It's adopting strategy-memes such as *Stay together, Provide for each other, Sacrifice,* and so on in order to preserve the marriage. It's adopting a whole set of association-memes connecting various feelings and ideas with marriage, commitment, and family. These days, it's common for two individuals getting married to have incompatible programming around marriage—conflicting strategy-memes or incongruous distinction-memes. A memetic marriage counselor would identify those and allow the couple to reprogram themselves with compatible memes.

Rapport and Mirroring

You're more likely to buy a dubious-looking meme, like a dubious-looking used car, from a buddy than from a total stranger, right? Well, a good salesperson knows that and will do everything possible to create a *buddy* meme in your mind.

How to create trust and rapport with a customer is one of the hottest topics in popular books and seminars on sales. The latest thing is to bypass your conscious mind and use NLP techniques to create rapport. Most people have no clue what's going on when salespeople do this, but if you know what they're doing, you can have some fun with them.

One basic technique is known as *mirroring*. If you're reading about this for the first time, it's going to sound really stupid, and you're not going to believe that anyone could do this ridiculous thing and get away with it, but believe me, it is done and it does work.

> Mirroring is simply matching someone's body language.

If she crosses her legs, you cross your legs. If she folds her arms, you fold your arms. If she tilts her head to one side and wrinkles her nose, you tilt your head to one side and wrinkle your nose. Sounds like fun, doesn't it?

Beyond simply matching posture, a good mirrorer will get a feel for the rhythm of people's movements, the pace of their speech, the texture of their conversational style. If you can match all that, you'll be like a perfect dance partner and develop that instant rapport usually known as *chemistry*. Yes, this works well for charming potential mates as well. The product sold most frequently throughout history has always been *yourself*.

Confidence Games

The masters of establishing instant trust and rapport are the people who run *confidence games*—con artists. "Con" stands for "confidence," and the game works by gaining your confidence in them and then tricking you. They work by creating a meme in your mind that says, *I trust them.*

There are any number of ways to create that meme: appearing naïve or innocent, performing a seemingly altruistic act, appearing to be part of a reputable organization. The most straightforward way, though, is by giving you *their* confidence first. By appearing to trust you, they hope you will reciprocate. Then they getcha.

One common con is the street game of three-card monte. The game appears to be simple enough. Three folded playing cards—two aces and a queen—rest side by side on a table. The dealer, a practiced prestidigitator who can make the cards fly around faster than the eye can see, shuffles the order of the cards. Players bet even money that they can pick out the queen.

The real game, however, is the mind game surrounding the card game. Here's one variation:

As you approach, you see what appears to be a player winning consistently against the dealer, picking out the queen and doubling his money every time. The dealer shuts him out, saying he can't play anymore, he's too good. Maybe they fold up the game and move a few steps down the street.

Intrigued, you continue to watch. Eventually, the former winner approaches you and whispers that he knows how to "find the lady," but they won't let him play anymore. He offers to give you some of his money, and if you bet for him, you can keep half the winnings. He'll whisper to you where the queen is—you can't lose!

After a couple of wins, he says he doesn't want them to catch on to him, but he thinks you can do one more hand. How much money do you have on you? Let's put it all down, yours and mine, and really soak these guys!

Well, why not? He trusted you—go for it!

When you lose everything, your new friend expresses shock and frustration. He is truly sorry. Just then, someone yells, "Cops!" and the dealer folds up the table and nonchalantly walks away. If you have any inkling of doing otherwise, there's a big, beefy guy who used to play nose tackle for the prison football team staring you down. You've been conned, my friend.

> Gaining someone's trust is an effective way to bypass their skepticism and make it possible to program them with new memes.

Viruses of the Mind

If you've been paying attention, you now know almost everything you need to know about how mind viruses work. Before you skip ahead to Chapter 11 and learn how to start a cult, let's take a moment to put all the pieces together and look at what we've got.

From Chapter 3, you know that a mind virus, or any virus, has three requirements: a method of penetration, a way of reproducing itself faithfully, and a means of spreading itself to other minds. When you have a concept or a subculture or a dogma that meets all these requirements, you have a mind virus.

> If you currently *believe in* any concepts or subcultures or dogmas that meet these requirements, and you didn't consciously choose to program yourself with these memes, you are infected with a mind virus.

If you're not aware that you currently believe anything like that, that doesn't necessarily mean you're not infected; it may just mean you're not aware of the infection. Here's what it looks like when you're infected by a mind virus:

Penetration

We looked at three methods of penetration: repetition, cognitive dissonance, and the Trojan horse. When a virus of the mind infects you, it may resemble one of these scenarios:

— **Repetition.** Repeating a meme until it becomes familiar and part of your programming is one method of mind-virus penetration:

- Hearing a similar message repeatedly on television news, commercials, talk radio, and so on

- Being in a group or organization where, for instance, a charter is read or an oath is taken at each meeting

- Hearing a point of view or opinion repeatedly—for example, about gun control or abortion (if you are not among the first to be infected, you could hear it from a wide variety of different infected people)

— **Cognitive dissonance.** Being placed in a paradoxical or mentally uncomfortable situation can lead to being reprogrammed with new memes that relieve the mental stress:

- Going through an initiation or hazing or a series of tests

- Taking a confrontational or uncomfortable seminar or course that gives a great sense of relief at the end

- Reaching some goal or reward after a struggle or after having been told you're not good enough

— **Trojan horse.** Bundling less-attractive memes with more appealing ones:

- Listening to a concept that mostly seems right but has a few components that kind of rub you the wrong way

- Hearing appeals to help children, resolve a crisis, feed starving people, and the like

- Being asked to believe something that seems odd just out of trust

- Being presented with an opportunity to get more or better sex or relationships by adopting some new beliefs

This is by no means an exhaustive list of methods of penetration by viruses of the mind. However, if you're looking to see what mind viruses you are already infected with, looking back to see which of these scenarios you've been through may give you some clues.

Faithful Reproduction

A mind virus needs a way to reproduce itself faithfully—without distortion or omission. That can be accomplished in a number of different ways:

- By instilling a belief that tradition is important. The way things have been said and done in the past is the way they will continue to be said and done.

- By saying a certain set of memes is the Truth, as many religions say about their sacred texts. Why would you want to distort or omit the truth?

- By setting up a structure to reward verbatim copying and/or punish modification. The military has such structures set up to condition people to reproduce the policies and procedures faithfully.

The eccentric spelling of the English language is preserved because of a pervasive meme that there are right and wrong ways to spell words. This meme has all kinds of support, including dictionaries, computer spell-checkers, and children's spelling bees. But before the *Use a dictionary* strategy-meme became prevalent during the 18th and 19th centuries, people spelled words any way they wanted. It's not True that there's one and only one correct way to spell a word—it's just a meme. As Mark Twain said, "'Tis a small mind cannot think of but one way to spell a word."

We *think* it's True because all our lives people have been criticizing us for misspelling words—we've been programmed. Not that there's anything wrong with consistent spelling—it enhances communication, after all—but it's important to start seeing that all of what we think of as the Truth is composed of memes, and most of those memes just came into our heads through programming, without any of our own conscious choice involved.

Any beliefs you have about there being a *right* way and a *wrong* way to do things can and will be co-opted by mind viruses as part of their faithful-reproduction machinery. Remember "a foolish consistency"! Consistency for its own sake is meaningless. Ask yourself if being consistent serves your underlying purpose, such as effective communication, or if you've just been programmed with a *Be consistent* meme, leaving you open to mind-virus infections.

Spreading

Spreading mind viruses is the flip side of penetration. This section is aimed particularly at the movers and shakers of the world. If you are an influential or vocal person, if you produce television shows, if you speak in front of large groups, if you raise children—I want you to be conscious of what memes you're spreading.

Naturally, a mind virus that infects people with memes that explicitly encourage spreading it will spread faster and more pervasively than one that just depends upon chance to spread itself. Some of the ways mind viruses encourage spreading are:

- Programming you with a meme like *Get the word out before it's too late,* pushing your *crisis* and *window of opportunity* buttons.

- Programming you with a meme to the effect that *teaching this to our children will help them.*

- Programming you to *evangelize* the virus. Some synonyms for *evangelism* are *proselytization, replacing yourself, passing the favor on,* and *enrollment.*

Evangelism has kind of a bad name in some circles. The paradox about evangelism is that in addition to being the mechanism used to spread mind viruses, it's also the main way people can have a positive impact on the world. You can have the world's greatest idea, but unless you shout about it, crusade—*evangelize*—it has no impact. *Virus of the Mind* is my attempt to consciously spread the bundle of memes known as memetics, which I see as essential to having our children live in a world of freedom, creativity, and personal power. I invite you to evangelize with me!

> *Evangelism* is the intentional spreading of memes. Make sure that the memes you're spreading are ones that you want the world to have more of.

A virus of the mind is a cultural institution that contains all these ingredients. It is therefore self-perpetuating and self-replicating—it continues through time and reaches out and involves more people. Institutions that were designed by people for the specific purpose of perpetuating and spreading, I call *designer viruses.* But long before anyone came up with that Machiavellian notion, viruses of the mind evolved on their own into powerful cultural fixtures. I call the institutions that evolved on their own to become self-perpetuating *cultural viruses.*

CHAPTER NINE

CULTURAL
VIRUSES

*"Society everywhere is in conspiracy against the
manhood of every one of its members. Society is a
joint-stock company, in which the members agree,
for the better securing of his bread to each shareholder,
to surrender the liberty and culture of the eater.
The virtue in most request is conformity."*

— Ralph Waldo Emerson

From the children's game of "telephone," we know that it's difficult to copy memes with 100 percent fidelity even if we want to. When replication occurs with slight changes in the replicator, and those modified replicators are selected somehow for their fitness, then we have evolution. When a concept appears that has all the properties of a virus of the mind, then as it starts spreading through the population, the memes constituting that concept evolve.

Toward what end do they evolve? We now come to the key to the paradigm shift: these memes, and the concepts and cultural institutions they compose, care nothing for you, me, or our

147

children except as vehicles for their own replication. They do not exist to raise our quality of life or to assist us in our pursuit of happiness. Their goal is to reproduce and spread, spread and reproduce, whatever the cost.

> All cultural institutions, regardless of their initial design or intention (if any), evolve to have but one goal: to perpetuate themselves.

Cynical? Well, maybe, but it's an inescapable conclusion from everything we've just discussed. Suppose you have 100 cultural institutions—let's take nonprofit organizations, for example. They have varying degrees of effectiveness in the charitable tasks they are designed to accomplish, and they also attract funding and volunteers in varying degrees. It is their effectiveness in attracting funding and volunteers that determines whether they can stay in existence and perform their functions.

After some period of time—say, five years—half of them go out of existence due to lack of effectiveness at funding or staffing. The other half either already possessed memes that attracted funds and staff or else evolved them during those five years.

Given the limited resources in the world and the new organizations being introduced all the time, the surviving organizations must become better and better at surviving. Any use of their money or energy for anything other than surviving—*even using it for the charitable purpose for which they were created!*—provides an opening for a competing group to beat them out for resources.

A friend of mine recently stopped donating to a wildlife-preservation group. Appalled by the volume of mail he received from the group after his first donation, he did some quick calculations. He realized that the cost of the mailings they sent him to solicit donations actually exceeded the annual amount he was donating! He sent the group a letter explaining why he was ceasing to support them.

If you're designing a cultural institution these days, you've got to know memetics. If you don't design the thing with good memes that will make it self-perpetuating from day one, it will either die out quickly or evolve to become self-perpetuating. The trouble is, the way in which it evolves could do great violence to the original purpose you intended.

In this chapter, I'll describe several types of cultural viruses—institutions that have evolved away from their original purpose and become self-perpetuating. In the next chapter, I'll explore the evolution of the biggest cultural viruses of them all: religions.

Television and Advertising

Television is a particularly efficient medium for meme evolution. New shows or commercials can reach hundreds of millions of people at once. If the shows catch on—if they have good memes—the producers are rewarded with inpourings of sponsors' money, the advertising agencies are rewarded with more business, and the sponsors themselves sell more of their product. All this happens relatively quickly, perhaps in a matter of weeks or months, as opposed to the old days when culture spread mostly by countries trading with and conquering one another over the course of decades or centuries.

Scares about so-called subliminal advertising have abounded in recent years. The idea is that unscrupulous marketeers have put hidden images, voices, or symbols into their ads for the purpose of manipulating people into buying products that they otherwise wouldn't buy. The story goes that one liquor company had an artist airbrush the word *sex* into the random arrangement of ice cubes in a glass, or that a cigarette manufacturer hid the word *death* in a waterfall, or that a seemingly innocent arrangement of random objects secretly formed a likeness of a naked and seductive woman.

This all raises a lot of questions, whether you see these images when you peer intently at the suspect ads or not.* But supposing subliminal images do exist, how did they get there? Are there really

---

*Personally, ever since I first read about subliminal advertising, I've seen the word *sex* in every glass of liquor on the rocks—now I've got a distinction-meme for it!

evil geniuses intentionally cackling over their airbrushes, manipulating and enslaving our minds? Or is the presence of these images
nothing more interesting than Charlie Brown's looking up at the
clouds and seeing a duckie and a horsie?

Of course, I don't know. But if we get stuck on that question,
we're falling into the biggest trap of all in understanding cultural
evolution. It's the trap that conspiracy theorists fall into, and the
same trap that people who pooh-pooh conspiracy theories fall
into. It's the mistaken belief that anything complicated must arise
out of conscious intention.

> Complicated things arise naturally out of the forces of evo-
> lution. No conscious intention is necessary.

Does subliminal advertising work? Sure! Ads can have parts
that you don't become consciously aware of but which draw your
attention unconsciously. If the ad pushes more of your buttons as a
result of the subliminal content, you will pay more attention to it.
Paying more attention is the first step toward paying more money.
It can work in reverse, too: some fast-food restaurants paint their
walls orange because they believe it creates subliminal discomfort;
you'll want to spend less time lingering there, and your leaving
opens up tables for new customers.

But don't think that subliminal ads are the only problem: as
should be obvious to everyone who has watched the evolution
of television programming for more than a few years, efforts to
attract your attention are not limited to the subliminal.

The television is *screaming* at us day and night with all the great-
est button-pushing memes there are: Danger! Food! Sex! Authority!
We don't even have to believe it's real for it to attract our attention.
Remember "I'm not a doctor, but I play one on TV"?

Not only commercials, but also programs are evolving to command a greater share of your mind, and to say they were doing
it subliminally would be an almost humorous understatement.
The first naked female breasts on American broadcast television

"There's nothing like a glass of Schroedinger's Vodka to help me solve hard physics problems!"

"Subliminal" advertising supposedly sneaks memes into your mind without conscious awareness on your part.

appeared on the program *NYPD Blue*. *Baywatch*, a show with little plot but lots of bare skin, became the most watched television show in the history of the world. Female breasts, naked or otherwise, tend to command men's attention, and hence, in the very efficient evolutionary medium of television, they tend to proliferate. A casual observer will notice that the inclusion of breasts, not to mention the rest of the female anatomy, in much male-oriented advertising is far from subliminal.

Advertisers have learned to push your buttons. They also have learned a good deal about programming you with all kinds of memes. It's not the subliminal that we need to be concerned with—it's that they now have the knowledge to unleash full-blown designer mind viruses through their advertisements. And the effects of that are unpredictable and frightening.

The Evolution of Advertising

Imagine it's 1960. Television advertising is in its tender youth. New York and Los Angeles abound with Darrin Stephenses working for advertising agencies run by Larry Tates, all trying different strategies and campaigns to advertise their clients' products successfully. They're all running their ideas up the flagpole, but only a few get the salutes required for success, promotion, and unabashed copying by everyone else in the business. It's a dog-eat-dog world, and the days where "I feed my doggie Thrive-O / He's very much alive-o!" can compete for a share of the viewer's mind are as numbered as those of the set shot in basketball.

Some campaigns work; some don't. The ones that don't are quickly killed, as few advertisers can afford to prolong an expensive promotion that isn't paying dividends in attracting the attention of customers and therefore their money. The ones that succeed are copied, with various creative changes being made intentionally or unintentionally—because the copier didn't understand what was effective about the original ad—yielding another generation of fitter ads. It's almost the reverse of the way some animals have genetically evolved camouflage to make themselves less visible: like colorful flowers evolving to attract pollinators, these commercials have evolved in the world of memes to make themselves *more* visible and attract *you.*

After several years, and without any evil top executives scheming about the best way to manipulate the American public, most ad agencies are putting out commercials featuring the big button-pushing memes: *danger, food,* and *sex.* Soon they start fine-tuning them, still through the automatic and unconspiratorial process of meme evolution, to include some of the other button pushers: helping children, listening to authority, the unusual, a sense of belonging, and so on. Ads could have evolved to where they are today simply through the natural process of competition, even if there were never an awareness on the part of ad-agency executives about the button-pushing effect these memes had on people.

Of course, there *was* an awareness of the button-pushing effect. In fact, advertising runs hand in hand with politics in its calculating manipulation of the masses. It's not clear to me that executives' awareness of the situation has much effect on the result, but it sure tends to make people think less of them. Even so, one can always give them the benefit of the doubt and still have a workable theory of meme evolution in advertising. Did the makers of Joe Camel deliberately set out to hook kids on Camel cigarettes by presenting a lovable cartoon figure smoking their instrument of death? Who knows? It does have that effect, according to at least one study, but that doesn't prove conscious intent.

It's a very, very attractive trap to start looking for who to blame for what people consider the decline of our culture. When culture evolves in the direction of more powerful memes, it does little good to single out people to blame. As you know by now, that's the natural order of things.

> If we want to combat the mind viruses responsible for the decline of culture, we need to be conscious of our own programming, consciously adopting memes that take us in the direction we want to go.

Things Go Better with Memes

Another effect of meme evolution on advertising is the divergence of advertising content from product content. As a kid, I remember noticing the Coca-Cola Company changing its slogan from "Drink Coca-Cola" to "Enjoy Coca-Cola" to "Things go better with Coke." Somewhere along the line, somebody realized that they didn't really have to discuss the product itself, just create a mood full of enough attractive elements that people took notice and felt good when they saw the product—they created an association-meme in the customer.

A '90s Diet Pepsi campaign featured celebrities and showgirls smiling, cavorting, and grunting "Uh-huh!" for half a minute. Not exactly a logical delineation of the product's features and benefits. The athletic shoes we used to call "sneakers" no longer get promoted by mothers swearing to the long life of the brand; now stroboscopic special effects surround famous athletes, poetic quotes, and rap music. Speaking of music, do you have a favorite song that has been ruined forever by an ad that used your enjoyment of it as a Trojan horse? Remember "I Can See Clearly Now"? I used to love that song, but now it just makes me think of Windex.

Advertisers are selling a feeling; they are using Trojan-horse techniques that hook into your feel-good buttons so they can unload their bundle of memes into your mind once they have your attention. In some cases, this transformation of commercials into direct communicators of powerful feelings has brought them full circle into the realm of art.

I'll follow up that little bit of blasphemy by pointing out that I have several friends who don't watch much TV. When we get together for the occasional viewing of some special program, it fascinates me that they are often more engrossed by the commercials than the program itself! It's as if, in order to sell products, the producers of TV commercials have made a return to the early days of television when a commercial consisted of little more than a mention of the product name. Many of today's commercials feature miniature dramas, comedies, music videos, or even experimental surrealism, completely unrelated to the products they're selling except for the mention of their name or a brief picture. It's a world within a world.

Beer commercials are notorious for this kind of treatment. "Sell the sizzle, not the steak," goes the advertising truism. Well, why not? When you're pushing a product made from rotten vegetation whose primary effects are to dull your wits, pad your paunch, and make you belch, any sizzle would be a big help. I remember a beer commercial from my childhood that sold the steak. It went:

> Schaefer is the one beer to have
> When you're having more than one!
> Schaefer's flavor just doesn't fade
> Even when your thirst is done!

What a nice ad promoting a true competitive advantage of the product. It even had a nice little tune you could hum. Now that's something that should really appeal to the connoisseur, right? Wrong.

Ever since Anheuser-Busch decided to bill its anything-but-outstanding Budweiser as the "King of Beers," the trend has been away from claims, true or not, about the product's competitive advantages and more and more toward building an image or mood.

> Advertisers want to program people to feel good and pay attention when they encounter the product.

The ads that push people's buttons are the successful ones. You don't have to have a Ph.D. in media studies to notice that sex plays a big role in beer commercials. But the competition is so fierce, and the payoff so great, that beer advertising has split off into surprising niches, exploiting some of our other buttons. The agency representing Budweiser and Bud Light now have the two square off in a confabulated "Bud Bowl" football game between two teams of animated cans and bottles every year during the Super Bowl, perhaps guessing that people paying attention to the real football game have particularly sensitive competition buttons, and so will pay attention to the commercials as well.

Stroh's beer ran a series of commercials exploiting a man's relationship with his dog. Rainier Beer, a local Seattle brew, had a very funny series of commercials that seemed to engender good feelings in the populace around the product. There was actual community outrage when the commercials were canceled by the new owners of Rainier. Henry Weinhard's beer ran a series of commercials exploiting the *tradition* meme, talking about their hundred-year history in the Northwest. Another Anheuser-Busch campaign slogan, "Proud to be your Bud," attempts to hook into people's sense of belonging and identity. There are still a few exceptional campaigns that actually talk about benefits of the product, such as

Miller Lite's innovative "Great taste, less filling," but by and large the beer industry is selling the suds, not the brew, as it were.

What does all this mean to you and me? It means that if we watch commercial television, we are guaranteed to be influenced in both our thinking and our behavior by the powerful memes being broadcast at us. Is that bad? I don't know. But anyone who claims television is not a great shaper of our culture is either naïve or mistaken. If television didn't have at least as great an effect on our behavior as one might suspect, advertisers would not pay billions of dollars a year to shape our buying habits. And shaped we are, both by the commercials and the program content.

Television Programs

The evolution of commercial television programming has been toward a combination of the memes that push viewers' buttons and the memes that people want to promote.* One way this shows up is in the phenomenon of the talk show.

While it might not be apparent to the casual viewer, most of the people who appear as experts or celebrities on talk shows are there in order to promote themselves or their agenda—to spread memes. To illustrate how important this is, a hardcover book generally needs to sell 5,000 copies in a week to make the *New York Times* bestseller list. A single appearance by an author on America's top talk show, *Oprah*, commonly sells 100,000 copies of a book. But you have to write a book that Oprah wants on her show. That may not necessarily be the book you want to write.**

There's no doubt that the visual media have influenced the publishing industry. Large advances go not to books with literary

---

*Douglas Rushkoff's book *Media Virus!* (Ballantine, 1994) illustrates this point in great detail. His use of the term *virus* is more like what I call a *Trojan horse*—that is, a bundle of memes with a sugarcoating of palatable memes and a hidden agenda underneath.

**As if to prove my point: one of my reviewers wrote in the margin here: "Be careful—don't alienate Oprah!"
I haven't, have I? ☺

value, but to those that are promotable—they have components that will push people's buttons. Top-selling fiction writers are more and more penning novels that read like screenplays. The visual adaptation of the book is far more lucrative, and reaches far more people, than the written version.

Cynics perennially ask why life and culture, and television in particular, seem to be filling up with valueless and demeaning junk rather than artistic and thoughtful content. The answer is, of course, that the valueless and demeaning junk is a better replicator.

> If you're interested in filling the airwaves with art and litera-
> ture, you've got to make them better replicators.

There are two ways to make something a better replicator: make it better exploit the environment, or change the environment to its advantage.

Using the first method, you could create art and literature that presses people's buttons, such as Robert Mapplethorpe's erotic photographs or MTV's music videos.

Alternatively, you could work to change the selection process for what goes on the air—not likely anytime soon in the United States, given how fundamental the free market is to U.S. culture. The difference in program content of the noncommercial PBS versus commercial networks shows what a difference the selective environment makes in determining what cultural replicators win the battle for survival.

One controversial method of making art a better replicator is the colorization of old black-and-white movies. While the additional visual appeal of color generates more viewers—or at least the meme *Colorization generates more viewers* has spread to the right people—colorization offends traditionalists, who especially resent tampering with films without the directors' permission. The director intended black and white, they say, to convey a specific artistic message. They warn that soon we'll see colorization of the first 20 minutes of *The Wizard of Oz!*

'My So-Called Life' axed over poor ratings

PASADENA, Calif. 11-Jan-95—Ten million viewers is not enough to save ABC's cult series "My So-Called Life," which finished ahead of only 16 other shows out of 116 in the season's first-half ratings.

The show will be pulled from the air Jan. 26, said Ted Harbert, president of ABC Entertainment, who called the critically acclaimed show "art" but said the show's ten million viewers were "a lot of people, but not so many people by our standards."

Explaining that he would be delighted to find a way to bring the show back, he said, "We're continuing to promote the hell out of it, trying to get an audience into it in these last few episodes in January."

While declining to predict whether the show would return in the fall, given the strong support of its core fans and critics, Harbert said he would make a decision in May, but that ratings were the key.

"None of these different fan groups are going to do a big job of swaying the network one way or another."

A critically acclaimed TV show can be a poor replicator if it doesn't meet the selection criterion for commercial television: ratings.

The most offensive example I've seen of tampering with artistic content for the sake of increasing viewership is the practice of showing a preview of a gripping scene in the next segment of the movie at the start of each commercial break. That's right—they show a scene you haven't seen yet, out of order, in an attempt to create sufficient interest for you to stick around through the commercials! Argh!

The point is, the institution of television, while originally created as entertainment, has evolved into a self-perpetuating cultural virus with little possibility of anything but broadcasting the most gripping, button-pushing sounds and images. That's true not only of the entertainment portion of television but also of the news.

Journalism

The idea behind freedom of speech, in the minds of the framers of the Constitution, was that if all ideas were given equal opportunity to compete in a sort of free market of the mind, the truth would emerge victorious. Unfortunately, this is not the case. It's successful mind viruses that emerge victorious, spreading their selfish memes.

> Truth is *not* one of the strong selectors for memes.

Making sense is a selector, since people have a drive to make sense of things, but as we know, that does not always correspond to truth. What laws govern our existence? Everybody understands the basics of astrology, which is not to say they believe it—but selecting one of 12 signs based on your birthday is easy to understand. That meme spreads much better than a more scientific theory such as quantum physics, in which the fundamental particles don't map easily onto people's birthdays.

All this makes life difficult for those heralds and guardians of the truth, those disciples of Benjamin Franklin: the news media. Constantly accused of bias and unfair reporting, members of this noble profession have a tough time balancing truth and objectivity against saying something interesting enough—pushing enough buttons—that people will listen to what they're saying.

Some journalists do not claim to report unbiased news. "Advocacy journalists" such as talk-show host Rush Limbaugh devote their airtime to promoting a particular point of view. Newspaper columnists such as P. J. O'Rourke do the same in the print medium. These people collect evidence to support their point of view, then put it out in an entertaining and button-pushing fashion in an effort both to gain converts and to increase their audience. Of course, the more buttons they push, the more people pay attention to them. As I write this, the *crisis* button is in vogue on talk radio, while the *helping children* button is a perennial favorite in print.

Newspapers typically put columnists in a special section called Opinion and Editorial (op-ed), advertising clearly the distinction between these "biased" pieces and the so-called unbiased rest of the paper. It's in the rest of the paper that the trouble starts. Because even if we grant that most journalists are good people of high integrity, the very assumption that it's *possible* to be unbiased is flawed. Having a nation of reporters running around believing they're unbiased and a nation of news consumers making the same assumption leads to lots of problems. More to the point:

> The whole news-reporting mechanism, with billions of copies of information being made every day, is a prime breeding ground for mind viruses.

It's considered sporting in the journalism field, outside of the op-ed page, to give equal space and time to opposing points of view so as to prevent biased reporting. The trouble is, in order to report effectively on something, it helps for the reporter to understand it. It's difficult or impossible, though, to truly understand a point of view other than your own, especially given the incredibly short deadlines most reporters have to write a story. And so without conscious intent, the opposing point of view will tend to get shortchanged.

Well, you might think, *Surely that will even itself out over the thousands of reporters in the country, each with his or her own point of view, right?* Not entirely. The culture of journalism is rife with mind viruses that have spread certain biases—certain memes— deeply throughout it, without any conscious intent on the part of individual journalists to be biased. Let's see how this works.

The very word *unbiased* implies that it's possible to report the news on some objective level separate from the reporter's own context of life. How practical is that? At the very least, the news media must decide what is important enough to be called news, and that judgment is inherently biased in several ways.

In the first place, any successful reporter is biased against the status quo. Why? Because nobody would go out and buy a newspaper that said, day after day, "Things are fine. Nothing to worry about." The *Things are fine* meme is a very weak one, not pressing any of our major buttons. We would ignore it; the paper would go out of business; the reporter would starve to death. *That* would be news!

Rumblings of a "liberal bias" in the news media during the Reagan and Bush, Sr., presidencies quickly turned to grumblings about "conservative hatemongering" when the more liberal Clinton was elected. Which one is true? Neither.

> In reality, the bias in the media isn't liberal or conservative—it is toward stories that push our buttons, meaning that we buy their papers, listen to their shows, and keep them in business.

One of the few voices for the status quo during the Reagan years was the show *Crossfire* on the Cable News Network (CNN). Brilliantly conceived, it set up a conflict between voices from the left and the right to press our *danger* and *crisis* buttons. With those memes penetrating our defenses, we heard both the liberal and conservative viewpoints.

The so-called liberal bias was not a "liberal" bias at all—it was a bias against speaking out in favor of the status quo, for a reason no more sinister than this: Being in favor of the status quo is boring! It doesn't push any Buttons. The news media have evolved into a self-perpetuating cultural virus speaking out in favor of change. This process has continued to the point where the word *conservative*—which used to mean "opposing change"—has evolved to refer to some of the most revolutionary ideas around! *Argue for keeping things the same* is not a good meme.

Conspiracy Theories

People's drive toward *making sense* of senseless things leads to a type of cultural virus known as a *conspiracy theory*. Over the years, people have suspected conspiracies in everything from the assassination of John F. Kennedy to the supposed plot by the American Medical Association to keep us dependent on medical care by limiting the potency of over-the-counter vitamins.

Do such conspiracies really exist on a large scale, or are they just isolated incidents such as Watergate, doomed to be uncovered because of the sheer difficulty of keeping a secret among so many people?

Larry King, one of my favorite talk-show hosts, regularly punctures callers' conspiracy bubbles by asking one question: *How could that many people keep that big a secret for so long?* "Sir, it just ain't possible," he concludes.

While he makes a good point about the difficulty of keeping good memes secret, that's really only part of the story.

> A belief system, through its memes, can spread in a way that looks just like a conspiracy without any conscious intention on the part of the participants.

Is there a conspiracy among America's farmers and the government to push meat and dairy products on us, knowing that the high fat content of those foods will damage our health? Nah, the farmers just want to sell their products to stay in business. Their lobbyists support politicians who see things their way, and pretty soon we've got television ads and government programs all proclaiming the benefits of eggs and pork, "the other white meat."

To the farmers and lobbyists there's no secret; they just want to make a living. But to someone who's not immersed in that culture, the message to eat meat and dairy products looks threatening, even evil.

How about the American Medical Association? Do they have a secret session at their annual meeting where they discuss ways

162

to cripple the American public to increase their business? Nah, they've just been programmed with the meme that they, as educated health specialists, are best qualified to regulate and dispense health care. From this core belief come policy decisions such as their stand on over-the-counter vitamins and regulation of nutritional supplements.

But don't conclude that conspiracies are impossible to keep secret. In fact, all but the most interesting conspiracies are extremely easy to keep secret, simply because news about them won't spread if it doesn't have good memes. A few years ago, the top three manufacturers of plastic dinnerware were found to have conspired to a price-fixing scheme. It was covered in a small article in the *Seattle Times*. What? You hadn't heard about it? That conspiracy was kept secret simply because most people had no interest in hearing about it—the story had bad memes.

It's incredibly hard to be heard. Businesses spend billions of dollars a year on public-relations agencies and advertising, trying to get their message out. Why would we think that a single leak by a conspirator would blow the thing wide open? It took many people working hard for many months to uncover the juiciest parts of the Watergate scandal, and that was an affair in the national spotlight.

Even that wouldn't have come out if Nixon hadn't taped himself doing illegal things. Why did he do it? Like the meat and dairy farmers taken to another degree, he was so immersed in his belief system, making the practicalities of reelection so important, that he simply didn't see himself as doing anything wrong. To him it wasn't a conspiracy; it was just a strategy meeting.

Like members of religions that practice ritual sacrifice of human beings, the Watergate conspirators had a set of beliefs that drove them to do things that mainstream America considered reprehensible.

> It's difficult to step out of your own memetic programming and see yourself as others see you.

In the case of Watergate, the American public, aided by the *Washington Post,* helped them do that.

You don't automatically pay attention to everything you see and hear. You automatically filter out things that don't coincide with your worldview, and that includes conspiracies, unless of course you're a conspiracy buff, in which case you tend to see them everywhere. It depends on your worldview, your context.

I wonder how long it will be before someone alleges a conspiracy among radio talk-show hosts, a conspiracy to pooh-pooh all conspiracy theories. How strange that so many of them automatically ridicule anyone who calls up with a new theory about the JFK assassination or the Trilateral Commission. Hmm . . .

Nah.

Man Bites Dog

It's an old saw of journalism that when a dog bites a man, that's not news, but when a man bites a dog—now *there's* news! The point, of course, is that everybody already knows dogs bite people: one more occurrence of this everyday event is not interesting to people. When something unusual or ironic occurs, though, people want to know about it.

This leads to another bias in the media: a bias toward the unusual and offbeat. It's only natural; people want to *hear* about the unusual and offbeat. However, the amplifying power of the media gives people a distorted impression of the world because the media rarely report the mundane and ordinary. We watch television; see crime, disasters, and superhuman athletic feats; and form a picture of the world having little to do with our day-to-day experience.

The problem is, going through life with a distorted picture of the world handicaps us.

In 1992, 37,776 people were killed by guns in the United

States. Another 40,982 were killed by automobiles.* Yet a casual look at reporting would verify that guns get much more coverage than cars, even though almost half the gun deaths (18,169) were suicides. I'm not saying guns shouldn't get more coverage—after all, this gun problem is new and growing, while the car problem has been with us for decades. But people get a distorted picture of the dangers involved.

Just doing a simple calculation, the chance of any one person dying in an automobile accident in a given year in the U.S. are 1 in 6,224; the chance of dying in a gun incident other than suicide is less than half as likely: 1 in 13,005. If you put yourself in a low-risk group by not being a criminal or a police officer, your odds get considerably better. But what are people more afraid of: guns or cars?

If you're like most people, the answer is guns, and it's likely because of the distorted media coverage. This kind of distorted coverage leads to an outcry from the populace, which often leads to politicians going off—forgive the pun—half-cocked with "solutions" to the problem.

Now let's get a handle on what it really means to have a 1-in-6,500 or a 1-in-13,000 chance of dying. It's as if you lived on an island in the South Pacific with a population of 650. You make your living by swimming around in the azure waters around your idyllic paradise and spearing fish for dinner. Yum, yum. About once every ten years, a stray shark happens by and eats a swimmer. That's a 1-in-6,500 chance of any one person being eaten by a shark, just the same as the odds of dying in an automobile accident in the U.S. in 1992.

Also, about once every 20 years, two men get into an overheated argument over a fish or a woman and one of them kills the other with his spear. That's a 1-in-13,000 chance of being killed in

---

*Source: "Advance Report of Final Mortality Statistics, 1992," from *Monthly Vital Statistics Report, Vol. 43, No. 6, Supplement,* March 22, 1995 (corrected and reprinted). U.S. Dept. of Health and Human Services, Public Health Service, Centers for Disease Control and Prevention, National Center for Health Statistics.

an argument, just the same as the odds of being killed by someone else with a gun in the U.S. in 1992.

These are very sad events, and probably dinner-table conversation for quite a few days, but not the be-all and end-all of life. Fortunately, since you live on an isolated island, these events come and go, and life goes on.

But now imagine there are 392,000 of these islands all linked by television and INN (Island News Network). This brings the total population to about 254 million, less than the U.S. today. Every night, INN reports on the goriest of the 107 shark attacks and 54 spear deaths *that day*. Suddenly people's picture of the world is quite different. From a peaceful existence disrupted only by a tragedy every few years, you go to a fear-ridden hell filled with crime and terror.

Isn't this interesting? Nothing has changed except the addition of television. Yet now it feels like you're living in a dangerous world, not an idyllic paradise. Same number of shark attacks, same number of spear deaths. What happened?

Television news. It's provided a new and powerful means of spreading memes that push our *danger* button.

> We're particularly susceptible to memes that push our *danger* button, since it was important in the days before television, back when the more quickly we responded to danger, the better chance we had to survive and reproduce.

But sitting in front of the television getting scared about danger halfway across the world isn't very useful and doesn't add much to our quality of life. It's like an addiction, a drug. We have very real buttons that get pressed when we see danger, buttons that drive us to pay attention to it. It takes substantial mental effort to pry ourselves away from it.

Back in our former paradise, people start demanding that the government do something about this new perceived danger. Politicians start talking about a five-day waiting period for spear purchases. Entrepreneurs start running half-hour infomercials for shark repellent. But underneath it all, the tragedy is that people don't enjoy life as much anymore. They live in fear, fear brought about by nothing more than television news.

Did it have to happen this way? What if the people who invented television news had decided to cover good, heart-warming news rather than scary, dangerous news?

For one thing, to stay in business, the news media have to report things that people are interested in. Those things are nothing more or less than memes that push our buttons. Now, silly us for having stupid buttons like *danger, crisis, power, territory,* and so on. But the fact is:

> Without appealing to those buttons, the masses will not tune in, and the network will go out of business.

If another network, say, TPC (The Peaceful Channel), were to go on the air competing with INN, showing sunsets, happy people, and palm trees blowing in the breeze, it would not be long before its directors would notice that certain shows got better ratings than others. Being committed to staying away from the *danger* button, they would have to find a niche with other buttons, maybe *food* and *sex*. Soon *The Island Gourmet* would go head-to-head with INN's *Shark Bite of the Week*. The search would go out for the perfect island woman guaranteed to capture the men's attention and make them dissatisfied with their mates' looks.

If it worked, and TPC did manage to capture some ratings points from INN, how long would it be before a competitor started a third network that put on shows that pushed not only the *food* and *sex* buttons but the *danger* button, too? Soon we'd have island soap operas and *Battle of the Volcano Virgins* capturing top ratings, and once again capturing our attention at the expense of our peace of mind and accurate view of the world.

You probably know people who are addicted to news, as well as other kinds of media stimulation. It's a drug of the mind, capturing your attention and giving little in return.

Turn off the tube.

Pets

Technology is by no means the only driving force behind cultural viruses. In fact, a cultural virus doesn't even have to be something bad. Take a look at pets.

> Our beloved dogs, cats, iguanas, and so on, along with the enormous industries that have arisen to support them, are all part of a huge cultural virus known as *pets.*

What? Pets, a virus? No, I'm not joking. Granted, from our egocentric point of view, pets are one of life's pleasures, delightful companions and playmates, part of the richness of being human. From their point of view, though, we're essentially their slaves. Let's take a look.

A virus of the mind is something out in the world that, by its existence, alters people's behavior so that more copies of the thing get created. Pets have all the qualities necessary to be a virus of the mind:

— Pets *penetrate* our minds by attracting our attention. The quality they have that gets them attention is something like "cuteness" or "adorability."

— Pets actually *program* us to take care of them in several ways. The animals themselves take advantage of the instincts we have to care for our young. The pet *industry,* part of the pet virus, programs us through television and advertising to spend more and more money on expensive pet foods and veterinary bills.

— Pets are *faithfully reproduced,* with the help, of course, of their own DNA and of the resources we devote to caring for them. But there's also a *tradition* meme working for many pet species in the form of pet shows and kennel clubs. People are rewarded for reproducing a breed faithfully.

— And of course pets *spread* in the natural way. They do this so effectively that we've noticed the problem and started campaigns to neuter animals to prevent unwanted offspring. Of course, eliminating unwanted offspring also increases the value of the faithfully bred animals sold by the pet industry.

Pets evolved to be cuter and cuter. How? The ones that weren't cute—that weren't able to command our resources, to enslave us into taking care of them—they died! It's natural selection in action: the cute ones bred with each other until we reached the point we're at today . . . infected with the pet virus.

Obviously, this is a bit tongue-in-cheek: nobody is worried about being enslaved by pets. But there is a species of ant that has evolved to literally enslave another insect, the aphid. The ants somehow evolved to give off the secret chemical that controls aphids' actions. The ants herd them, graze them, and milk them, much as we do with cattle.

Pets don't give off a secret chemical, but they do have an irresistible cuteness that serves much the same function. So next time you see a dog or cat, just for a minute look at it from the animal's point of view. Pets have got a pretty cushy life, don't they?

Panhandling

People in big cities don't give many handouts to beggars anymore. There's a sense that the people begging aren't the ones who really deserve the help. The "business" of begging is just as subject to memetic evolution as all other institutions. It seems the ineffective beggars—probably those you'd want to help—have been driven out by the ones who've learned to be good at it. Panhandling is an interesting study in meme evolution: like the progression of the forest, it seems to re-evolve over and over again each time a new environment is created where panhandlers can flourish.

Being "good at" begging, in this book anyway, means having the right memes to attract donations. Laws being passed against aggressive panhandling show that a *Be aggressive* strategy-meme has been successful. Other strategy-memes I've noticed working for beggars are *Beg with children or animals, Stand at a busy intersection with a traffic light,* and *Have a sign saying "Will work for food."* I actually heard a beggar on talk radio comparing techniques, and he highly recommended the last two of those three. He noted that he'd never actually worked for food—people just handed him money through their car windows, especially middle-aged women.

With "pro" beggars using such effective memes, it's difficult for the amateurs to get attention, and therefore donations. From an embarrassing but necessary way of life, begging has evolved into a cultural virus that perpetuates itself through ever-more-effective methods now being spread even over mass media.

> The most effective participants in this virus make a fair living at it, according to their own statements, and drive out the people who actually need help.

This force of meme evolution, away from original intent and toward exploitation of the system, works just as surely with government handouts, be they welfare programs or tax breaks.

Government

Power corrupts. No doubt about it. Federal bureaucracies grow fat and wasteful; politicians cater to special-interest groups or worse; big businesses shower ineffective executives with lavish salaries and fringe benefits. We know about all of this, and many of us have grown jaded and grudgingly accepting of this black eye on the face of society. We catch them when we can and toss them out of office or even into jail for a few months, but it's just a fact of life, isn't it? Power corrupts.

What I once thought was a cynical, pessimistic worldview, I now understand to be the natural result of meme evolution.

Mind viruses exploit instruction-obeying mechanisms. If power is defined as the ability to have others follow your instructions, it's not a difficult leap to see why evolutionary forces tend to attack and corrupt any concentration of power.

The very instant we set up a bureaucracy, a government, or a big business with extraordinary power over our lives, corruption begins. Little by little, the good intentions originally present in the organization become stifled, choked, or even replaced by an evolving set of memes that have no claim to power other than that they are good at spreading.

The forces of meme evolution are unbelievably powerful. Take a look at that unshakable bedrock of government: the U.S. Constitution. Ratified in 1788 and designed by some savvy people with firsthand knowledge of the corruption possible in a big centralized government, it contained many provisions devised to safeguard against that happening in their new country.

But little by little, and always for what seemed to be good reasons, power shifted from the people and states to the federal government. Did you know the original Constitution prohibited the direct taxation of people by the federal government? The IRS was unconstitutional! The framers knew that with centralized taxation comes centralized power and centralized corruption. And what we see through memetics is that such a central power is doomed to evolve away from any charitable intent and toward self-perpetuation.

The United States has evolved so far away from the ideas of individual responsibility and states' rights that people now puzzle over the meaning of the Tenth Amendment. It says that all rights not specifically granted to the federal government shall be reserved for the people or the states. That's still part of the Constitution! The power of meme evolution has brought us to an era where the federal government sees nothing wrong with mandating a national speed limit, controlling access to health care, and deciding which drugs people will be imprisoned for using and which will be subsidized by the taxpayers.

The Black Market

Whenever the government outlaws certain forms of economic activity, it creates the potential for a cultural virus called the *black market*. A subculture springs up full of strategy-memes such as *Sell drugs* in order to reap the rewards. These black-market memes push some of the primarily male buttons discussed in Chapter 6—*power* and *window of opportunity*—so one would expect primarily men to be involved in black-market activity.

The so-called war on drugs, in a parallel to the former prohibition of alcohol, created a niche of enormous power for a group of people who are now necessarily outlaws, the black-market drug dealers.

The more difficult the government makes it to acquire illegal drugs, the higher prices black marketeers can charge. The harsher the penalties for dealing drugs, the more freedom the dealers have to commit other crimes in their pursuit of the economic and social power their trade gives them. After all, they're already criminals and have little more to lose: *low risk, high reward*. The tighter the crackdown by the government, the scarcer the supply of drugs, and the more potential for money and power individual dealers have: the more strongly the *window of opportunity* and *power* buttons get pushed.

As we discovered during Prohibition, the good the government does by reducing drug use must be weighed against the harm done in supporting the criminal underground that serves this black market, not to mention the loss of individual freedom caused by the state imposing its group morality on everyone.

So why does the government have a "war on drugs," knowing that it creates this black market and all the crime that goes with it? It's the chief disadvantage of a democratic government, especially in this age where national offices are determined mostly by television coverage.

> To get elected, leaders are forced to advertise themselves using the most powerful memes available.

Lately, this has involved pointing out a *crisis* (the drug problem, the budget deficit, health care, our broken educational system). Unfortunately, the effectiveness of the button-pushing memes in the campaign sound bites is unrelated to whether the proposed solutions will actually work to solve these problems.

A Democratic Republic

The framers of the U.S. Constitution understood this problem, and that is why they created not a true democracy but a republic: the citizens democratically elect representatives, and then they— presumably the elite thinkers, the people of highest integrity— make informed decisions based on what is best for the country.

What happened? Meme evolution, this time mutating government toward the direct vote of the people, who ultimately hold the reins of power. In 1913, another article of the Constitution fell, again with noble motives, this time the one providing that state legislatures would nominate senators. Now it would be the people, thus removing the distinction the framers designed into the two-house system, with the House of Representatives being the voice of the people and the Senate being the voice of the states.

The so-called smoke-filled rooms, where candidates used to be nominated, for better or worse, by the local party powerful, have been eliminated in state after state in favor of direct elections, thus ensuring that any successful candidate would have to distill his or her message into a short ad that pushes a lot of buttons. Cries are now being heard to eliminate the Electoral College, the last smidgen of power individual states have in affecting the Presidential election, in favor of a direct national vote.

At this point, I'm not trying to say that evolution of the government toward more and more centralization is a bad thing—although it *is* a bad thing for people who want to have control over their own lives. Rather, I'm just showing another example of the way systems automatically evolve toward the powerful getting more powerful. The more power an institution has, the more it can influence the spreading of its memes. The more it spreads its memes, the more power it gets.

Article I, Section 3

The Senate of the United States shall be composed of two Senators from each State, chosen by the Legislature thereof, for six Years; and each Senator shall have one Vote.

17th Amendment (1913)

The Senate of the United States shall be composed of two Senators from each State, elected by the people thereof, for six years; and each Senator shall have one vote.

✳

Article I, Section 9

No Capitation, or other direct, Tax shall be laid, unless in Proportion to the Census or enumeration herein before directed to be taken.

16th Amendment (1913)

The Congress shall have power to lay and collect taxes on incomes, from whatever source derived, without apportionment among the several States, and without regard to any census or enumeration.

Original limitations on government power in the U.S. Constitution have eroded, giving more and more power to the federal government and to the majority voters at the expense of legislators and states.

> In the United States, the majority voters have the ultimate power, so we see slow but noticeable evolution toward what is called the *tyranny of the majority:* the majority imposing its memes on the minority.

The Bill of Rights was designed to make such tyranny impossible. Yet without a single one of those first ten amendments being repealed or modified, their enforcement and interpretation has shifted bit by bit to take power away from the individual and give more and more to the majority.

This shift in power always seems to be for a good reason at first. For instance, the right of people to hire and rent to whomever they choose has been overpowered by the government's attempt to eradicate the effects of sexism and racism. While the short-term results, better treatment of women and minorities, appeal to the majority of voters, the long-term increase in government control over yet another aspect of life is not so appealing.

One of the most precious rights, one that gives Americans cause to call their country "free," is the right to due process of law before the government can seize property. Current government policy against suspected drug dealers is to seize cars, boats, and houses used in drug crimes even before the suspects are brought to trial and convicted. Is this a good policy, or one more example of reaction to a short-term *crisis* by increasing central power?

The Origins of Gridlock

This corruption of government is rarely a conscious, evil intention on the part of the powerful. When it is—when a powerful leader abuses the trust placed in him and commits illegal acts— we can recognize the problem easily and mete out punishment swiftly when the crime is discovered. It's more difficult to deal with what we see all over the world today: the gradual infection of the entire power culture with memes that divert the power away from the purposes for which it was initially granted.

Let's take the U.S. Congress as an example. The original concept was for wise people to make informed decisions about the course of the new country. They would decide how much to tax citizens, how much to spend, what to spend tax revenue on, and what regulations to create.

> The very instant this power structure was brought into existence, it laid itself open to attack by mind viruses.

Any memes that infected legislators and shifted their priorities got some very powerful results. Not only are politicians powerful people, able to act on those ideas, but they are notorious talkers and tend to spread the ideas they're promoting through speeches and other means.

At first, legislators picked up ideas from reading, listening to others, and perhaps from offhand conversation in social circles. The political views that had the best memes—that appealed to the legislator for whatever reason, whether it be *crisis, helping children, making sense,* or some personal button—were the ones he adopted. But pretty soon, with all the memes buzzing around the legislator's ear, there began to be some fierce competition for his attention.

Regardless of their merit, memes needed to come in more and more powerful packages to win the notice of the legislator. One powerful package is a package wrapped in money: campaign contributions to the legislator's biennial need to get reelected. It's easy to pay more attention to the memes of groups that contribute than those that don't, and paying attention is the first step toward meme penetration. Even if the legislator is completely honest, the contributor's memes have their penetrating effect.

A corporate lobbyist or special-interest group, bringing up a matter again and again, would use *repetition* to advantage in transmitting memes to legislators. Today, legislators are surrounded by lobbyists, people employed solely to transmit particular memes to legislators—to condition them, to program them with memes! The legislators, in turn, hire huge staffs to sort through all the information coming in and screen it. The lobbyists now must figure a way to penetrate this new layer of defenses in a sort of congressional arms race.

This wouldn't be anything worse than inefficient if it were not for one key fact: the legislator's job is *not* to select the best ideas from among all the special interests' proposals; it is to decide what is best for the country! The vast majority of the memes that congresspeople are being bombarded with are requests to directly or indirectly benefit some interest. It's almost impossible for them not to be biased in favor of doing *something*, enacting *something*, regulating *something*, to address these issues.

When Good People Have Bad Memes

Put the special-interest bombardment together with the way our political process works and it's easy to reach the conclusion that espousing special-interest memes is a necessary condition for being in Congress. This does *not* mean that these people are bad or evil. It's just the forces of meme evolution.

Suppose a politician were to shield himself from the meme attack somehow and remain devoutly committed to doing what was best for the country. Unless he translated that course of action into memes that appealed to voters, that person wouldn't stand a chance at reelection against an opponent who tapped into the current hot buttons of the majority of voters, regardless of what was best for the country.

Pretty soon, the only politicians in office are the ones who are broadcasting memes that push voters' buttons. And it could all have happened through meme evolution, without any conscious intention to deceive or manipulate.

> Politicians win elections based on the only factor that counts: voter appeal, which is to say good memes.

Elective government is set up to select for politicians who are good at saying what people want to hear. And the more important television becomes in political advertising, the less related this political image becomes to the reality of the person. Today, only the most foolhardy or reckless Presidential candidate would make a television appearance without advice from a "handler"—an image advisor—to instruct him in how to come across most effectively.

Growth of Government

Despite the admonition, often attributed to Thomas Jefferson, *That government is best which governs least,* democratic political systems have evolved toward government governing more and more. That evolution is a result of the memes that voters pay attention to.

There is a tendency to notice the *reward* meme—to vote for politicians who make an issue out of doing something that benefits you as a voter. As a student, I remember activists mobilizing in favor of candidates who promised to increase government spending on education and student loans. The "pork" that members of Congress bring back to their home districts gets them votes, but it all adds up to a burdensome amount of federal spending and an ever-increasing amount of power in the federal government.

To unseat an incumbent, a challenger must send a message with better memes than the incumbent's message. Often that message involves bigger or more expensive government. The trend of all this has been for the U.S. government to get continually bigger, fatter, and more expensive and inefficient, while the memes used in the campaign get leaner, meaner, and more potent.

Meme evolution, though, is difficult to predict. The 1994 U.S. election saw a message filled with *mission* and *danger* as the Republicans took over the House of Representatives and the Senate over the Democrats' *stay-the-course* message. "There's a crisis!" they said. "We can fix it!" They managed to package their "Contract with America" platform with essentially the same button-pushing Trojan horse the Democrats used in 1992 to promote their solution to the then-hot "health-care crisis."

> As politicians become more and more adept at button pushing, the outcome of the election becomes less and less related to their real agendas.

If the majority of voters understood memetics, would we see a sudden transformation? We would certainly see a change for the better in the types of campaigns and, perhaps, the integrity of government.

CHAPTER TEN

THE MEMETICS
OF RELIGION

*"I like your Christ, I do not like your Christians.
Your Christians are so unlike your Christ."*

— Mohandas Gandhi

It's been said that believing in a Christian God is an obvious choice: if He exists, the penalty for nonbelievers is substantial; if He doesn't, what's the harm? This argument presses our *cheap insurance* button and feels like a good one. But, shamelessly biased as I am in favor of reality, I'm going to at least explore the possibility that religious beliefs are not in fact handed down from on high, but are instead the result of some of the most powerful mind viruses in the universe.

I'm writing now about religious dogma. I'm addressing the question of why people have religious Truths they believe, where such beliefs come from, and how they perpetuate and spread. People relate to religious scripture anywhere on the spectrum from vehement disbelief to useful allegory to word-of-God fundamentalism; and while the memetics behind the spread of such scripture is the same, the behavior of someone who is programmed with dogma-as-Truth is very different from someone who sees the same writings as a parable, a mythology.

You can consciously program yourself with memes that help you with whatever you're up to in life. That's one of the main strategy-memes in the memetics paradigm. It goes against that strategy to believe religious dogma without having consciously chosen it as empowering to your own life. It's also counter to the memetics paradigm to believe religious memes or any memes are True, rather than half-truths useful in a given context.

> The long-standing religious memes around today are the ones that survived memetic evolution. Like any memes, you get to choose whether programming yourself with them aids or hinders your life purpose.

The Origin of Religion

Where did religious memes come from? Here's one possible scenario. It's the era of prehistoric man, and problem-solving skills have turned out to be a big win in the survival-of-the-fittest game. The cave people who survived to reproduce were the ones who evolved to answer questions like:

- How do I hide from this saber-toothed tiger?
- Where is the food?
- How can I find Mr. or Ms. Right?

You know, the typical day-to-day concerns of the sophisticated cave dweller.

Problem solving was a good survival skill. But once that mechanism came into existence, early humans naturally turned it to some of the big problems, the ones philosophers throughout the ages have been struggling with:

- Where did we come from?
- Why are we here?
- What should we do?

Well, these questions were a lot harder to answer than the more practical ones involving danger, food, and sex, but not so hard that our Stone Age friends couldn't venture a guess. The cognitive dissonance set up by having these questions in mind caused the creation of some memes that made sense as answers. And from these guesses evolved mythology, philosophy, and religion.

How did that evolution work? As always, survival of the fittest memes. Without going into the actual history of religion, let's continue our imaginary Stone Age scenario. Imagine the Flintstones and the Rubbles are all pondering the question of where we came from. Each comes up with a guess: Wilma concludes God created us, but keeps it to herself. Barney thinks about the question for years, but the poor lunkhead doesn't come up with an answer. Betty, thinking about the question with exceptional insight and creativity, proposes that we evolved from single-celled organisms. Needless to say, Betty's idea doesn't catch on.

But Fred, who is more than middling pleased with himself that he has solved this stumper, figures we were created by God, Who also told us to spread the word or we'd burn in hell.* Yabba dabba doo!

Fred happened to come up with a fit set of memes in his guess at the solution to the problem. Did he do it on purpose? Almost inconceivable. But imagine millions of people all thinking from time to time about this question, and the set of beliefs constituting the accepted answer constantly "improving," evolving to have better and better memes that spread farther and wider and more rapidly, until the belief system pervades the society and becomes a religion.

---

*Current religious history places the invention of the *hell* meme with the Jews under Roman oppression. It was not then tied to evangelism; it was thought to be an explanation of why God would let the Chosen have it so much worse off than the Gentiles—the Romans might have it good right now, but there would be hell to pay later. Hell is only a minor part of Jewish dogma. It really caught on with the Christians when, combined with the *evangelism* strategy-meme, it became imperative to spread Christianity and thus Save the unbelievers.

A religion formed in this way, as a cultural virus (evolved without conscious human intention), evolves not toward truth, not even toward the betterment of its adherents, but toward *more effective memes*. This is the most crucial point in this entire book:

Meme evolution is not designed to benefit the individual.

So for religions that were not created by individuals with the conscious intent to start a designer mind virus—which I would imagine accounts for most of the religions on Earth—the belief systems are not guaranteed either to be True or to be good ways to live life. They are, however, guaranteed to be self-perpetuating.

When I say there was no conscious attempt to start a designer virus, I don't mean there was no conscious attempt to spread memes that would yield a good life. It would seem that many religious leaders, from Buddha to Jesus, did have a conscious intent. But without knowledge of memetics on the part of their founders, those memes either died out or quickly evolved into self-perpetuating institutions, concerned more about their own existence than about people's quality of life. And many of the religious institutions did so by claiming that their memes were the one set of True memes, regardless of the intention of their founder.

The Absolute Truth

When I was growing up, one of the typically adolescent questions I pondered was, *With so many religions on Earth claiming to be True, and many of them claiming to be the only Truth, how could I know which one really was true?* There didn't seem to be any easy way to tell: it seemed most of the world religions looked upon people of other faiths with attitudes ranging from indifference to pity to disdain, but usually with superiority and a smug belief that theirs was the only True way. And then there were the few that didn't make that claim: was one of *those* the true one? Who to believe?

One of the biggest traps people get into in life is getting sucked into trying to solve perceived problems at the expense of things that are more important to them. The *problem-solving* tendency in many of us is so strong that, without a solid grounding in and clear understanding of our own personal priorities, we tend to devote much of our lives to solving problems that don't get us anywhere. How to make more money, how to change our spouse's behavior, how to conquer fears: these perceived problems stare us in the face every day and therefore are each fodder for countless best-selling books, talk shows, and seminars.

But the biggest problem-solving trap that even highly educated, brilliantly intelligent people fall into is the Quest for the Absolute Truth.

> We have an enormous hunger to understand the world around us, which was extremely useful when the world was simple and mostly consisted of physical rewards and dangers. In the society of memes, however, we are constantly trying to make sense of things that simply *have* no sense.

We *think* they make sense, because our brains haven't had much of a chance to evolve from the time when these cultural, psychological landscapes simply didn't exist. So we devote huge amounts of time, money, and energy trying to understand and solve meaningless problems.

The biggest meaningless problem is this: Which religion is True? That breaks down into subproblems such as: Does God exist? What is He like? Is there a heaven? Is there a hell? Was Jesus Christ the Son of God? What does God want me to do? Then those break down into even more meaningless questions: Is God a man or a woman? White, black, red, yellow . . . ? Where does He or She live? How much postage does it take to send Him a letter? When He's on vacation, does He have His mail forwarded? How many angels can dance on the head of a pin?

Immersed in questions like that, it's difficult to get a perspective on what religion is and where it came from. But from the memetic model, all naturally evolved religions—cultural viruses—are bundles of memes. Religions are creations of our minds, kluges that have evolved from the days when our lives were mostly spent avoiding danger and seeking food and sex. Religions are conceptual bundles that map the prehistoric world our brains were used to onto today's world of morals, culture, and society. And unless we *invent* our own religion—a designer virus, with a particular purpose in mind—the way these bundles shape up is determined by meme evolution: religions evolve to have good memes.

That's it! That's all there is to it! None of the religions is the True one; they're all variations on a theme—or a meme. But let's take a closer look at what memes make for a successful religion.

Religion Memes

If I'm correct about religions evolving to have fit memes and not being handed down from God, I'd expect all our favorite memes to show up in the most successful religions. So let's take a look. Let's start by looking at the structural memes, those that are fit simply by virtue of the laws of memetics:

— **Tradition.** The *tradition* strategy-meme replicates because it programs people to perpetuate itself—along with the rest of the bundled memes. Religions have among the strongest traditions of any cultural institutions. From Mecca, ancient churches, and Eastern monasteries to kosher laws and the careful preservation of the Bible, traditions pervade most religions. Remember: It's not that the traditions are being kept because the religions are true or good—the cause and effect are reversed! The religions survived because, in part, certain traditions became ingrained in them. Religions without strong traditions had less chance of surviving.

— **Heresy.** Heresy is any belief that goes against the dogma of a religion. The flip side of *tradition,* the *heresy* distinction-meme is like an infection-fighting white blood cell, identifying and combating infectious new memes. Heresy carries with it a whole list of association-memes about what will happen to you if you believe (allow penetration of) or speak (spread) heresy.

— **Evangelism.** The *evangelism* strategy-meme replicates because it's shouting "Spread me to new people!" This one is interesting because not all religions are evangelistic in the sense of standing on street corners handing out pamphlets. But you'd have to look hard to find a major religion that doesn't evangelize to the children of its adherents. This works even better when combined with the *Have as many children as possible* meme favored by the Pope, Mormons, and our current welfare system.

It's beside the point that people are sincere and have good reasons to evangelize: "Jesus/Scientology/The Forum/The American Way made such an incredible difference in my life that I want everyone else to experience that joy." The institutions that encourage evangelism—that even *condition* people to evangelize—have a memetic advantage, regardless of the impact of the religion on people's lives. The religion is successful *because* somehow evangelism became a part of its dogma. A religion that gave people incredible joy but did not program them to evangelize would not be as successful.

— **Making sense.** Ideas that make sense replicate better than those that don't by the very nature of the human mind— remember the children's game of "telephone." Religions that have clear, handy explanations for those tough questions are much more popular than those that challenge people to think for themselves, such as Zen. Of course, those answers to tough questions don't have to be *true,* any more than Santa Claus or the Easter Bunny, as long as they're easy to understand.

— **Repetition.** Rituals abound in most religions, from Sunday church to saying grace before meals. The more we repeat an action, idea, or belief, the more comfortable we get with it and the less we question it: we become conditioned or programmed by it. Successful religions have evolved to embody what any advertising executive would tell you: repetition sells.

A strong dose of each of those memes alone would make for a successful religion, but meme evolution didn't stop there. Now let's look at the push-button memes, the ones that are fit because they take advantage of our basic human nature:

— **Security.** Many religions are based in fear: fear of God's wrath, fear of burning in hell, fear of ostracism by one's community. Setting up artificial dangers and claiming to be a safe haven from them is a very powerful part of a belief system. In the case of ostracism, the danger is not even artificial: the Amish live in fear of being "shunned," or cut out of their close-knit community for the rest of their lives. Living within the entire belief system of the religion is the supposed salvation.

— **Crisis.** Many cults, not strong on pushing the *making sense* button, make up for it here. Cult leaders Jim Jones and David Koresh were both said to be constantly trumpeting imminent danger, both from God's wrath and from outside enemies. They alone held the key to salvation in the crisis—so they said.

— **Food.** Yes, food! Feasts and fasts make a religion more attractive by hooking into people's most basic button. I almost joined the Baha'i faith once because I thought it was great to have feasts every 19 days!* Easter dinners, Passover seders, and the times you get to eat during the fast of Ramadan all add attractive memes to a religion. Fasts, in fact, set up cognitive dissonance to reinforce the memes you were fasting *for.*

---

*You have to believe before you can eat: feasts are for Baha'is only.

— **Sex.** It's the rare religion that doesn't have something to say about sex. To be an effective component of a belief system, though, getting the sex must be tied in with buying into the rest of the belief system. Religions have various ways of accomplishing this, from monogamous marriage within the church to the temple prostitutes of ancient Rome to the free-love cults such as the Rajneeshees. When the Rajneeshee enclave in Oregon started to get regular visits from sold-out tour buses full of salivating men, the Bhagwan Shree Rajneesh decided to put a ten-day waiting period on sex with newcomers, a small memetic change that made it less easy to snatch the bait out of the trap, as it were.

— **Problem.** This one is especially pernicious and effective at lassoing in smart, educated people. The idea that there is a mysterious body of knowledge that can be attained through a lifetime of problem solving is a powerful lure. This is the cornerstone of such Eastern religions as Zen and Taoism, although adherents would probably tell you it isn't. (That's what makes it so mysterious!) Religions such as Christianity have so much written about them that you could never make a dent in it in a single lifetime. But for many Christians, religious study is a great part of their lifestyle. They pore over the Bible, believing it is the direct word of God, bringing enlightenment if they could just understand a little more.

— **Dominance.** Having a status ladder to climb is great for hooking people with strong *power* buttons, which are mostly men, since this button is evolutionarily linked to access to females. The idea of levels or degrees runs through even quasi-religious organizations such as the Boy Scouts and the Freemasons. It's interesting that the Catholic Church, with one of the shortest ladders of hierarchy—only five levels from laity to Pope—exclusively addresses men and explicitly requires celibacy to move up the ladder. Perhaps celibacy tricks the mind into enhancing the drive to climb the ladder.

— **Belonging.** Most people have a button that draws them to belong to a group. For many lonely people, this meme by itself is sufficient to get them involved in whatever religion happens to be handy and holding regular meetings. I know several Unitarians who profess not even to believe in God; they just like going to church and meeting with their group.

Science vs. Religion

Although memetics makes it breathtakingly clear how religions have evolved, it does *not* force us to conclude that religion is a bad thing. That's a knee-jerk conclusion often reached by people when they discover that memes have been the driving force behind the success of religious dogmas, and it's a very shallow conclusion. On the contrary, memetics may help bring science and religion back together after a centuries-long falling-out.

The gap between science and religion began practically with the origin of science. Religious teachings have been at odds with scientific theories for ages. With each new one of its discoveries, science calls further and further into question religious histories and explanations. Many scientifically minded people can't understand why anyone would want to believe in something obviously untrue, or even believe something you don't *need* to believe in order to explain how the universe works.

Most intelligent people I know have divided themselves into two camps when it comes to religion: On one side, they either become agnostic or atheist, unwilling to buy into what they see as impossible stories of supernatural powers, virgin births, parting of seas, or other miracles. On the other side, they adopt a religion and become adept at rationalizing the "truth" of such stories* or treat them as allegorical mythology rather than Truth.

So we're at a bit of an impasse. Many of the religious *know* they are getting value from their faith: they see and feel the tangible results in their lives. Many who shun religion *know* they are right: their understanding of the world makes it obvious to them that these mythologies are just fairy tales, and why would anyone want to believe a fairy tale? And so the two groups stand on opposite edges of a chasm, shouting across at each other or turning their backs on each other, but rarely making the leap across.

To the Greater Glory of God

A common belief among the deeply religious, if you ask them the purpose of their lives, is something along the lines that they devote their time on Earth to the greater glory of God. What does that mean? For one thing, it means that they are clear that there *is* a purpose to their lives, something most faithless people are not at all certain about.

But so what? A harsh if typical attitude from the rational, scientific community might be something like this: "I really pity those poor religious fools who run around like chickens with their

---

*There's even a fellow who travels the world lecturing about how the theory of the origin of species through evolution couldn't possibly be true—sort of religious disinformation! I watched one of his lectures on television, enjoying the challenge of finding the holes in his logic. It went something like this:

"Look at all the beautiful colors of birds! There's no scientific reason for them! They're just beautiful! Obviously the work of God!"

"Look at how complicated the eye is! Couldn't have evolved! Must be the work of God!"

"The dinosaurs got wiped out for no apparent reason! Science can't explain it! Looks like the work of God to me: they probably got caught in the Flood!"

(I suppose they were too big to fit in Noah's ark.)

If the logical holes in this argument are not immediately apparent, and you enjoy scathing attacks on creationism, read Richard Dawkins's *The Blind Watchmaker* (Norton, 1987).

heads cut off, devoting their lives to bring 'glory' to a god that doesn't exist." And of course, the faithful look back in return at the godless empiricists, pitying them for never knowing the rapture of Grace.

Usually, what scientific-minded people object to about religion is an overdose of *faith*—believing in something without any evidence, or even despite evidence to the contrary. They point to the Crusades and the Spanish Inquisition as examples of how destructive faith in the unscientific can be. This always puzzles me since, as scientists, they should know you can't prove a theory by citing a couple of examples, especially when there are plenty of examples of good stuff created by people as a result of their faith, and bad stuff created by the faithless—and by scientists, for that matter! The officially godless Soviet Union and weapons of war spring to mind as an obvious case in point. I'm not saying that all the scientists who work on weapons are faithless, just suggesting that their faith is not a driving force behind their work.

But take a look at some things that were a result of faith: most of the great architecture, art, and music throughout history! We'd be much poorer without the Sistine Chapel, *The Last Supper,* or Bach's "Jesu, Joy of Man's Desiring." America was built on the Protestant work ethic, and the revolution that created the United States is based upon the recognition of God-given rights. Most charities serving the poor and helpless are religious organizations, which function far more efficiently than government welfare programs. Even the most hard-line empiricist cannot avoid recognizing the *results* of faith.

> The reason faith in God works is that when people believe they have a purpose to their lives, they get things accomplished that they otherwise wouldn't.

The beliefs (memes) you happen to hold at any given time program your mind to work in certain ways, much as loading a program into a computer causes it to perform certain tasks. If you program yourself with the belief that life is meaningless and random, you are likely to live a meaningless and random life. If, on the other hand, you program yourself with the belief that there is a purpose to your life, you will tend to accomplish that purpose.

The self-fulfilling strategy-meme of having a purpose to life is one key to why religion works. Now, if you object to swallowing a volume of fairy tales just for the sake of having a more fulfilling existence, I don't really blame you. But don't labor under the assumption that your *current* picture of the way the world works is accurate either. We all live with a certain amount of delusion and self-deceit; maybe it's just a matter of consciously picking the right set of delusions to point us in the direction we want to go.

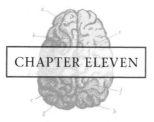

CHAPTER ELEVEN

DESIGNER VIRUSES
(HOW TO START A CULT)

"The first man who, having fenced in a piece
of land, said, 'This is mine,' and found people
naïve enough to believe him, that man was
the true founder of civil society."

— Jean-Jacques Rousseau

Throughout history, there have always been those who would manipulate others in order to gain sex, money, or power. We have not yet put that era behind us. The new science of memetics provides extraordinarily powerful tools for manipulation: designer viruses that, once unleashed, self-replicate and channel people's lives toward some self-serving end. Unlike cultural viruses, which simply evolve to perpetuate themselves, these Machiavellian designer viruses serve their creators' agendas.

Now, if I was the only one who knew about these, I might not write about them. Why put more tools in the hands of the bad guys? Why risk going down in history as the new Machiavelli? I've already had a few cautions from people who fear what will happen when this technology becomes well known.

But the point is, there are already designer mind viruses out there. Telling the whole world about how they work is my attempt to level the playing field. In the same way you'd warn an innocent young virgin about a slick suitor with a philandering reputation, I feel compelled to expose the hidden workings of designer viruses. My intent is to help people keep themselves from being taken advantage of, from being unwittingly programmed by designer-virus memes.

The memes we're programmed with drive our behavior. That's why mind viruses are so scary and powerful. If it were only a matter of getting infected with some silly meme like *The moon is made of green cheese* and going ahead and living a rich, full life with that mistaken knowledge, it wouldn't be a big deal. After all, if you ever got to the moon, you'd find out it wasn't made of green cheese and say, "Oh, isn't that interesting." No biggie.

But our memes drive our behavior, and when mind viruses infect us with memes that cause us to act in ways that derail us from our pursuit of happiness, we have a problem. *Virus of the Mind* is an urgent attempt to alert people to that danger.

In this chapter, I'll explore what life will be like in the new era of designer viruses, examine the ingredients that go into their design, and speculate on a few that may already be with us.

Viruses of the Future

In the not-so-distant future, the bulk of our culture will be composed of designer viruses. Why? Because now that we know how to design them, we will. We will conquer the conceptual landscape as surely as we conquered the wilderness. At first, designer viruses will compete with cultural viruses for a share of our minds. Soon the old cultural viruses will lose, because the natural selection with which they evolve is not as quick as the intelligence-directed creation of designer viruses. Those ways of thinking won't be wiped out completely, but more and more people infected with old cultural viruses will be restricted to self-contained, incommunicado enclaves like the Amish.

After that battle, designer viruses will have to start competing with each other, and increasingly sophisticated technology will be needed to create a winner in the mind war. We will see computer programs doing sophisticated memetic modeling to fine-tune the memes before launching.

What kinds of designer mind viruses will we see in the future? It depends upon the intentions and the skill of their creators—and on the memes those creators are infected with! I would expect to see many profit-motivated viruses, many power-motivated ones, and perhaps a few motivated by someone's vision of a better future for humanity.

Profit Viruses

Profit-motivated designer viruses, many of which are completely legal and aboveboard today, have their shady origins in the crooked Ponzi scheme.* Charles Ponzi was an Italian immigrant who opened a business in Boston in 1919 called the Securities Exchange Company. He offered to repay people's investments in 90 days with 50 percent interest: an investment of $10 would bring $15 in three months.

His story was that he bought international postal reply coupons in Europe and, due to currency fluctuations, redeemed them in the United States at a profit. People started to get suspicious when a newspaper discovered that, with $15 million invested in Ponzi's firm in eight months, only $360 in postal reply coupons had been sold—in the entire world!

Ponzi's scheme was simple: as long as his base of investors kept growing, he could pay off early investors with the cash pumped in by later ones. When the newspaper story broke and people stopped investing, Ponzi was found to owe $7 million and have only $4 million in assets. The later investors were out of luck.

---

*An entertaining exploration of Ponzi's original scheme and several other interesting virus-like phenomena appear in Joseph Bulgatz's book *Ponzi Schemes, Invaders from Mars, & More Extraordinary Popular Delusions and the Madness of Crowds* (Harmony Books, 1992).

The mind virus in the Ponzi scheme, though, had nothing to do with the scheme itself. It was the spreading of the strategy-meme *Invest with Ponzi*. Bundled with powerful button-pushing *window of opportunity* and *reward* memes—a *Get rich quick* meme—Ponzi's scheme attracted so much attention that it spread quickly throughout the general public in Massachusetts and neighboring states.

Ponzi's exploits were fraudulent on the face of it: he was lying to people about what they were investing in. But the related *pyramid scheme* had no requirement to lie to investors—its memes worked with complete honesty. In a typical pyramid scheme, there is an organizational chart in the shape of a triangle, with one name at the top; two names on the level beneath that; two names beneath each of those two, for a total of four on the next line; and twice that, for eight, on the last line.

The player whose name is at the top of the chart holds a "pyramid party" for new recruits. The bottom row, with eight spaces, is blank, and the host is hoping to fill them. Players are recruited to buy memberships for, say, $1,000. Of that fee, $500 goes to the person at the top of the pyramid and $500 goes to the name in the row of four directly above the new player's. You recoup your investment quickly, simply by recruiting two new players.

When all eight spaces are filled, the host, who recouped his $1,000 long ago when he was in the row of four, retires with a profit of $4,000. The pyramid then splits in two, with the two players in the row of two each becoming hosts eligible to make $4,000. Such a deal!

Pyramid schemes rely on the same button-pushing memes that the Ponzi scheme does and add in the powerful force of *evangelism*. Since infected people have a stake in enrolling new players in the pyramid virus, the illusion of reward doesn't need to be as great as with the Ponzi scheme. Rather than simply attracting new investors, there is now an army of recruiters intentionally infecting people with the pyramid virus.

Although the pyramid virus's spreading mechanism is different from the Ponzi scheme's, the two institutions fall apart for the same reason. Dependent on exponential growth, they quickly exhaust the supply of players. The initiator of the pyramid needs to enroll only 14 people to make his $4,000; after ten pyramid splittings, new recruits to the row of eight would need to enroll 14,336 new players, for a total investment of $14,336,000, in order for all of them to cash out.

When you saw "profit viruses," did you immediately think of Amway? Amway is the most successful of the currently proliferating profit viruses known as *multilevel marketing* (MLM). Multilevel marketing is distinct from a pyramid scheme and is legal. Instead of selling memberships that have no value except that they give you the right to sell more memberships, MLM creates a pyramid-shaped network of distributors of an actual product. *Upline* distributors receive a percentage of the sales from the *downline* distributors whom they recruited.

For an honest MLM business to work, the members' rewards should be based on their success both at selling the product and at recruiting new members. Large profits go to the relatively few people who, through persistence and good salesmanship, build a large and successful organization underneath them. Their financial reward comes at the expense of many people who join, expend some energy, and decide it's not for them.

It's a business of equal opportunity and survival of the fittest! In some ways, you could look upon MLM as morally superior to traditional businesses with relatively unchanging organizational structures. In traditional companies, those at the top tend to stay there, making large profits at the expense of low-level employees with relatively little opportunity for advancement.

Multilevel marketing is the business of the future. As broadcast media and the competition for the consumer's mind become costlier, noisier, and more crowded, the opportunity to sell directly and cheaply through a multilevel network grows more and more attractive.

Example of a Pyramid Scheme

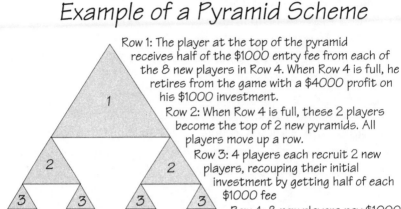

Row 1: The player at the top of the pyramid receives half of the $1000 entry fee from each of the 8 new players in Row 4. When Row 4 is full, he retires from the game with a $4000 profit on his $1000 investment.

Row 2: When Row 4 is full, these 2 players become the top of 2 new pyramids. All players move up a row.

Row 3: 4 players each recruit 2 new players, recouping their initial investment by getting half of each $1000 fee

Row 4: 8 new players pay $1000 each to join the pyramid.

A pyramid scheme, like this one, is an example of a profit virus.

> The key to a successful profit virus is having an incentive to *evangelize* or *enroll* new people.

A few years ago, the MCI telephone company introduced a hugely successful profit virus called "MCI Friends & Family." Subscribers got the largest discount on phone calls to their friends and family, but only if they *enrolled* them in the program. Brilliant! With a small burst of advertising to seed the program, it had the potential to take off on its own.

The MCI Friends & Family program ran into trouble because of AT&T's belated response. The telephone giant spent what must have amounted to tens of millions of dollars blanketing the airwaves with anti-MCI ads. These ads created negative association-memes with MCI's program and promoted AT&T's deal, which gave you discounts whether or not you enrolled people.

In response to AT&T's campaign, MCI had to look in a new direction. If they had understood memetics, though, they might have decided to stick it out or even add better memes to the Friends

& Family program. You see, AT&T would have needed to keep advertising forever to counter MCI's self-perpetuating profit virus. While AT&T may even have had a better deal, they did not do as MCI did and harness the exponential force of self-replication, the most powerful force in the universe.

Power Viruses

Someone once said a cult is a religion that hasn't caught on with enough people yet. I disagree with that definition, but not in the way you might think: I don't think a cult has to be a religion at all. There are two key elements necessary for a cult:

1. Each individual commits to some mission or higher purpose not chosen through personal, conscious reflection.

2. There are serious consequences attached to leaving.

These two memes—*commitment to mission* and *consequences of leaving*—are sufficient to harness people's lives and labors in a cult. When combined with some form of *evangelism,* a powerful mind virus is created, a *power virus* that spreads automatically as far as it can throughout the population.

A cult is a kind of power virus. The whole point of the thing is to give power, in the form of access to money, sex, and/or people's energy, to the cult leader.

> When cult members devote their life energies to a purpose outside themselves, that gives power to whatever the external purpose is.

The word *cult* is usually reserved for organizations considered evil or harmful by the masses, but the workings of power viruses are identical whether the purpose of the organization is moral, immoral, or amoral.

Cults typically have a mission that they say they're working toward—perhaps a holy mission. Members are conditioned to believe this mission is the most important use of their lives, and they should be willing to sacrifice everything else for the higher purpose. Once that meme gets programmed in, they're effectively enslaved.

If you're currently dedicating your life to a mission or higher purpose, I would suggest you reconsider your dedication based on three tests:

1. If you were asked, "What is the most important use of your life?" would your answer be that mission?

2. Does evidence show that your participation with this group is really the most effective way to fulfill this mission?

3. Do you have a personal sense of fulfillment from your day-to-day participation with this group?

If your answer is no to any of those questions, what the heck are you doing there? If you found the questions difficult to answer, I'd say you're in great shape. If it was easy for you to answer yes to all three questions immediately, you've almost certainly been programmed, and you should at the very least take a break from what you're doing and go smell the fresh air for a while.

Ever-growing megacorporations are power viruses, and they are beginning to use designer-virus techniques to grow more and more powerful. In a free-market economy, it's not surprising to find corporations making better and better use of memes to further their economic ends. Like all meme evolution, this can happen without any conscious intention.

> The companies that try out strategies that effectively harness memes simply do better and get copied by others.

It has become popular in corporate America for companies to design *mission statements* and ask or require employees to subscribe to them. These are typically straightforward and nonthreatening bundles of corporate values such as "commitment to quality" and "devotion to customer service."

What's the purpose of a mission statement? It's to get everybody pointing in the same direction so each employee's work builds on the others'. Without that alignment, people tend to work more at cross-purposes; they may find their efforts cancel one another out rather than add up to something significant.

The idea of aligning people's intentions is so successful that a whole economy has sprung up around corporate training seminars designed to do just that. When does this corporate training cease to be training, though, and begin to be conditioning, programming, brainwashing? When you're immersed in such a culture, be it a cult or a corporation, it's difficult to discern whether the group's mission is really the best use of your life. *Is it?* It's a good question to be asking yourself consciously.

Another meme-harnessing strategy used by corporations is called *golden handcuffs*. The gold these handcuffs are made of is a financial reward, usually in the form of stock options, that is tied to the employee's long-term participation with the company.

> Golden handcuffs are nothing more than the *consequences of leaving* meme, the same one used by cults to keep people in line.

Another method of bonding people to an organization is the cognitive-dissonance effect of the initiation ordeal. By putting people through a trial by ordeal such as a fraternity hazing, one of two things occur: either the initiate leaves rather than endure the pain, or a meme representing the value of belonging to the organization is created or reinforced in the initiate's mind.

After being initiated, members of a fraternity feel a bond to the organization and an irrational sense of value in belonging, a sense they wouldn't feel as strongly if they hadn't had to go through the ordeal to get there.

While corporations rarely use hazing, in many professions there is the concept of *paying your dues,* going through a period of time where your duties are somewhat unpleasant and difficult before moving on to a more enjoyable position. This effectively brainwashes you into believing that your current job is more valuable than you would otherwise think.

Youth gangs typically have initiations involving committing a serious crime. These serve a dual purpose: the programming or brainwashing effect of cognitive dissonance, and the assurance that the initiate has bought into the lawlessness of the gang culture.

I used to watch a lot of television. I don't anymore, but one of my favorite shows was an episode of *Family Ties* in which Alex, the teenage archconservative, falls in love with a girl who's a liberal activist. In order to get close to her, he attends meetings of her organization and even goes so far as to prepare a speech arguing against everything he previously stood for.

While Alex eventually came clean and told her the truth before it was too late, I wonder how many of us start down the path of our political beliefs for similar reasons?

> Beliefs are like cow paths. The more often you walk down a path, the more it looks like the right way to go.

After a few years of thinking liberal thoughts and making decisions based on them—poof! You're a liberal! It's much more difficult and energy-consuming to start from scratch on every issue and really think it through than to attempt to be consistent with a particular set of beliefs.

This is where Ralph Waldo Emerson comes in again, saying, "A foolish consistency is the hobgoblin of little minds." I often surprise people with what they perceive to be a lack of consistency in my points of view. Good! It means I'm staying off the cow paths!

I wonder what would happen to someone like a Kennedy or Dole if they magically got appointed to the Senate for life and no longer had to be mouthpieces for the Left or Right. It's not so far-fetched, actually. There have been any number of Supreme Court justices who have surprised everyone by voting more liberally or conservatively than their Presidential appointer had presumably hoped, once they got their lifetime position. Their barriers to leaving their ideologies were removed, and they were free to think for themselves.

> When you get people to commit to a belief system and put up barriers to keep them from changing their minds, you've effectively harnessed their lives and energies. Add evangelism and you've created a self-spreading power virus, using up people's lives to achieve some end.

Alignment of purpose is not necessarily a bad thing—just make sure the purpose is one that you consciously subscribe to, that's honestly accomplishing what it says it is, and that's personally fulfilling. Microsoft, where I worked for a long time, had a clear mission from the beginning, one voiced by the company's co-founder, visionary genius Bill Gates: a computer on every desktop, and Microsoft software on every computer. Beneath this major mission were a bundle of values* shared by everyone in the

---

*Working at Microsoft worked well for me for many years because I shared those values personally. I like to be a kind of special agent who comes in and saves the day. In fact, with Microsoft's fantastic success I felt like they were doing so well that they didn't need me anymore. That loss of a sense of purpose contributed to my losing interest in working there and finally taking the leap to becoming a writer and teacher. Before I left, though, I considered jumping on board their new consumer division, a place where the challenge of going from zero to market leader once again materialized.

company: technical excellence, intolerance of shoddiness, highest quality, and above all, being number one.

I wouldn't bet against them.

Virus Shells

If you really want to start a cult or some other virus of the mind, you now know everything you need to do it. Just find some attractive memes to suck people in and program them to do your bidding, including evangelizing the cult to others. But watch out! It's the virus of the mind that *really* has the power, not you. Remember Jim Jones and David Koresh.

It's interesting that once you have the shell of a successful mind virus set up, you can just plug in any agenda you have as long as it doesn't interfere with the virus's primary function of self-replication. There are many examples of such virus shells in modern life:

— **Political campaign organizations.** These often use the same basic formula: renting a vacant shell of office space, calling people and asking them to volunteer, and then having those volunteers call still more volunteers. The volunteers self-replicate, and you can plug in literally any political agenda.

— **Multilevel marketing companies**, as described earlier in the chapter. The product sold is really secondary to the structure of the business. Of course, you need to have a real product to make it legal, but it's effectively programming members to recruit more members that makes it work.

—**Word-of-mouth seminar series.** Participants attend a several-day, intensive seminar that leaves them feeling very good. Mixed in with the course content is the use of conditioning, cognitive-dissonance, and Trojan-horse techniques that program people to do two things: recruit new participants for the next offering of the class; and sign up for the next, more expensive seminar in the series.*

The common thread in all mind-virus shells is evangelism. Directly or indirectly, you've got to recruit members who recruit more members who recruit still more members. When you've got a good virus shell, you can plug in your agenda, cross your fingers, and hope it doesn't mutate to come back and getcha.

Quality-of-Life Viruses

In a future where mind viruses proliferate, the kinds I personally want to see win are viruses that raise people's quality of life. The way to make such viruses win is twofold:

1. Evangelize, evangelize, evangelize! When you come across memes you like, spread them consciously! Silence is death to memes.

2. Make a point of tying together all the button-pushing memes you can with the memes that raise quality of life. Point out how they help our children! Remind people this is a crisis! Serve them food! Offer them sex! Well, whatever. But complacency is defeat in the world of mind viruses—you're competing with all these self-replicating memes designed to take us back to prehistoric times.

Is all this evangelism and button pushing I'm promoting too Machiavellian for your taste? Does it sound hypocritical, like I'm advocating manipulating people to save them from being manipulated? I hope not. I don't want you to lie, just to understand

---

*Don't read this to mean that all such seminars are scams. I can say unequivocally that taking at least one seminar series that uses this virus shell was one of the most valuable learning experiences of my life. Unfortunately, I've also been acquainted with a few that are genuine cults. My advice: before you take one of these courses, ask the advice of someone you trust, who has a life you like, and who has not been involved with the organization for at least three years.

the effect you have on the world by spreading memes. We're all participating in mind viruses all the time. I want you to choose which ones you spread consciously, with an eye toward what's most important to you.

James Redfield's best-selling *The Celestine Prophecy* is an effective mind virus. It's a fictional account of the author's discovery of an ancient manuscript—one that purports to contain a prescription for a rosy future for humanity. Now I don't know if Redfield did this intentionally or not, or if he's even aware of it, but he put a mind virus in that book—a good one! I'll tell you exactly how it works.

One of the lessons of the Celestine manuscript is that there are no coincidences. All seeming coincidences are actually opportunities for growth. In particular, when you find something coincidental about people, you have a duty to talk with them until you find out what the lesson is that either they have for you or you have for them. People who read *The Celestine Prophecy* absorb that meme and start looking for such opportunities. Naturally, that often turns into a recommendation to read the book—to evangelize it! Presto! A mind virus is born.

One aspect of Redfield's advice is actually terrific and touches on the main advice I give in this book:

> Take any opportunity to spread the memes you want to have out there.

I'm not a particular fan of all of the memes in that book, but whenever the subject of *The Celestine Prophecy* comes up, I sure turn it into an opportunity to tell people about memetics. "That's really interesting," I say. "Did you know there's a virus of the mind in that book?" And I go on to have a lively discussion about mind viruses.

One quality-of-life virus known to be created intentionally—a designer virus—is The Hunger Project. A spin-off of Werner Erhard's personal-growth groups *est* and *The Forum* (evangelistic designer viruses themselves), it makes no pretense of doing any-thing other than spreading its own memes. All The Hunger Project does is educate people that there is a problem with world hunger and ask them to commit to ending it. The group buys no food, sends no money to the poor, plants no rice—all they do is hold seminars at which they enroll people in the project and raise money to enroll more people.

It might at first glance seem that this is a useless pursuit. But don't underestimate the effects of spreading memes. The effect of enrolling several million people in a commitment to end world hunger may be substantial—they may go off on their own and cause something to happen out of that commitment. They're certainly more likely to do so than if they had *not* made the commitment.

In any case, this designer virus has been successful thus far judged solely on its ability to replicate: millions of people have gone to a Hunger Project event since its inception.

Ending world hunger is a worthy end, but I'm willing to be even more ambitious. How about a designer virus that disinfects people from mind viruses and inspires them to live the most ful-filling life possible? How would you launch such a virus? Could you be sure that it wouldn't mutate into something undesirable? In the next chapter, I discuss the nature of disinfection.

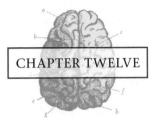

CHAPTER TWELVE

DISINFECTION

"If only he had used his genius
for the forces of niceness . . ."

— Maxwell Smart, the protagonist
in the TV show *Get Smart*

Scientific revolutions often bring with them profound philosophical questions. The memetics revolution is no different. We can't even talk about disinfecting ourselves and society from mind viruses without bringing up two very important ethical questions.

Here's the first: I've named this chapter "disinfection," but given that our minds are made up of genetic hardware and memetic software, what does it even mean to be disinfected? Certainly not to wipe out *all* of our memes! What memes do you want to be programmed with? This is the classic philosophical question: *How should I behave?* brought to a new level: *How should I program myself?*

The second ethical question is one already being pondered by psychologists and NLP practitioners. What memes do you want to program other people with? *What memes should I spread?* The knowledge that you can actually have a huge impact on other people through the memes you spread carries with it a correspondingly huge responsibility.

What Comes Naturally?

Many people's immediate reaction is not to want to think about these questions. "That's so artificial," some say. "I'll just take what comes naturally," speaks the gut feeling. Careful—remember what that "gut feeling" serves!

> Your "gut feelings" evolved to maximize your DNA's chance of replicating back in prehistoric times.

Never thinking about these ethical questions is, of course, one way to deal with them. If you do that, you're leaving evolution in the hands of selfish memes, which evolve according to the tendencies we developed in the Stone Age to support our selfish genes. There's absolutely no incentive for meme evolution to provide for our happiness. Infestations of mind viruses that chain us to information terminals, frantically aiding the replication of information, may well take over if we don't intervene.

Do you think it's a far-fetched scenario of the future that humans could become slaves to a race of computers? Look inside any large office building and see how many people spend eight hours a day following the instructions on their display screen to the point of damaging their vision and injuring their hands from the strain. What are most of them doing? Entering, duplicating, correlating, and analyzing information. Memes. When we aren't working, we're telling each other about the latest news, probably something to do with danger, food, or sex. Memes.

No, memes aren't *automatically* going to evolve to benefit our survival, let alone our happiness. Meme evolution is on a completely different timescale from genetic evolution—a much, much faster one. We have no choice but to confront it or let it rule our lives. If we want to direct meme evolution in a way to benefit our species, life on Earth, or anything, we're going to have to take the bull by the horns. Punting on these two ethical questions—admitting defeat—just keeps the infection going.

> We can either give up on the hope of having a fulfilling life and a better world or consciously choose which memes to program ourselves with and which we want to spread.

Of course, many people *do* punt on these ethical questions; most aren't even aware of them. Thoreau said, "The mass of men lead lives of quiet desperation." Why? It doesn't seem to make sense—as beer drinkers know, we only go around once in life, so why don't we grab all the gusto we can?

Because it really feels like you *have to* follow these programs that have been stuck into your head by mind viruses! Until you break free, it's tough to realize that life can be different, that you're allowed to figure out what's most important in your own eyes and devote your life to that.

Curing this infection, both in ourselves and in others, is going to take a conscious effort. It won't happen automatically. If we just kick back and watch TV, we will probably not evolve in a way that you or I will approve of. The future of our world will not look good. Even if you and I cure ourselves, unless we act to spread the cure to others, we and our children will end up living in a world where people are living less and less meaningful lives. They will devote more and more of their lives to being the unknowing slaves of mind viruses. We've got to act now.

Think about your personal answers to the two preceding ethical questions. Try some of the ideas in the rest of this chapter to disinfect yourself. If it calls to you, be the new champion of childhood education, and we can begin to teach children how to guard themselves from infection. Imagine what creativity and contribution would be possible in the world if children grew up able to make the most of life's opportunities!

In this chapter, I'll start by discussing the first ethical question: *What memes should I program myself with?* Then I'll outline some methods for recognizing your current programming so that you can break free of the mind-virus infections you currently have. Finally, I'll open the question of what memes we might want to put out into society, and especially to the next generation of children.

The Quest for Truth

What memes should you program yourself with, now that you have the chance? The second-most-popular answer (after punting) is: *With the truth.* It's hard to see how there could be any problem with programming yourself with memes that are true. But remember Alfred North Whitehead: all truths are half-truths.

There are several problems with the strategy-meme *Program myself with the truth.* In the first place, you can't ever know the whole truth of the universe. Your brain doesn't have enough storage capacity to accurately model the entire universe. The best you can do is come up with some simplified models that work most of the time. To paraphrase Whitehead, it's believing these models are true that plays the devil!

In the second place, it's often distracting and time-consuming to find the truth past a certain point. The use of instant replay in America's National Football League (NFL) is a perfect example. Recognizing that even the best officials made mistakes, the NFL owners decided a few years ago to have an additional official watch the game on television. In the case of a questionable call, he would stop the game, view replays, and possibly overturn the field official's decision. The replay official, having an opportunity to view the play slowly and from different angles, would have a better chance to make a correct call—to know the truth!

In 1995, NFL owners voted to end their experiment with instant replay. They decided that stopping the game and interrupting the fans' enjoyment wasn't worth the additional truth they got from the process. They saw the trade-off between enjoying life and knowing the truth and decided in favor of enjoyment. They have since resumed the use of replays on a much more limited basis.

People programmed with the *quest for truth* meme often spend time analyzing past events, trying to figure out who was right, who was wrong, what people's true intentions were, and so on. Like stopping the football game for instant replays, stopping to figure out the "truth" all the time can distract from your enjoyment of life.

Finally, the "truth" is always based on some set of assumptions—memes. Until you've really mapped out your memetic programming, you're not aware that you even have these underlying memes making certain things look true. In my experience, the more you understand your own memetic programming, the less anything in life looks like the Absolute Truth.

So, besides *what comes naturally* and *the truth* as meta-strategies for programming yourself, what else is there?

Serving Your DNA

You could devote your life to the replication of your DNA. This has never been an attractive option to me, but you *could* make *Serve my genes* your meme-programming strategy. For women, this would mean having as many babies as you could support, which in most civilized countries means as many as you could physically bear. For men, it means impregnate, impregnate, impregnate! Throw out those condoms! Get out your Yellow Pages and start dialing up sperm banks! Travel a lot, and secretly have three or four families in different places! That is, if you're really serious about serving your DNA.

But why serve only the DNA in your own body? Why not serve all human DNA? Or, for that matter, all animals, all insects, all bacteria, all—viruses?

If you're going to serve your DNA, remember: *what comes naturally* no longer works. You're going to have to think. It may not always be what feels the best. You're going to need to be conscious of having that purpose for your life and program yourself for it. But if you're going to pick a life purpose, serving DNA seems like a silly one to me.

A Life Purpose

The people I've met who seem to be getting the most out of life are those who have some kind of life purpose. Now, there are an infinite variety of life purposes; and in fact there are plenty of cults, corporations, and other mind viruses happy to give you one that serves their *own* purposes. I would suggest you select a "higher" purpose for yourself that maximizes your fulfillment and enjoyment in life.

Psychologists and psychiatrists such as Abraham Maslow and Viktor Frankl have noticed that when people are willing or forced to stop worrying about such issues as their own survival and imminent crises, they have another set of drives, referred to alternately as "higher purpose," "calling," or "self-actualization." Where did these drives come from? People will split over two possible answers to that question. Some will say they come from God. Others will believe these higher drives are "just there" in our brains as artifacts of evolution—klugy side effects of DNA that in some other way support their own replication. Fortunately, either point of view works equally well to continue exploring how they relate to memes.

These drives seem to be even more varied among different individuals than the second-order buttons described in Chapter 5. Helping people find their calling or purpose in life is extremely rewarding for me and is one of the goals of my first book, *Getting Past OK,* and of my *Your Life's Work™* seminar. These drives constitute what some people call spirituality; they are by definition drives to live life in the way that each individual would consider the best use of his or her time on Earth.

> When they have the presence of mind to see beyond the day-to-day hassles of life, people hunger deeply to fulfill whatever is their own personal life purpose.

Mind viruses leech our lives away from that purpose. Most of us are unwittingly infested by these unwanted parasites on our lives. Let's find them and exterminate them so we can make the most of our lives.

Zen and the Art of Devirusing

Although Zen masters never heard of the word *meme*, becoming aware of the memes that program one is the essence of the Zen discipline. There is incredible value in learning how to free yourself from the prison of thoughts and mind programs anytime you want to.

Zen practitioners meditate and ponder riddle-lessons called *koans* in an effort to retrain their minds to do just that. They learn to take in exactly what their senses perceive and to dissolve the artificial distinction-memes of human ideas and concepts. As any adherent of Zen would tell you, it's almost impossible to even understand what this means unless you've actually done it.* Successfully practicing Zen is said to produce an extraordinary feeling of peace and clarity. It would seem to be one method of curing yourself of mind viruses, if you're willing to spend 20 years practicing (or if you're in a hurry, as one Zen story goes, *30* years).

However, Zen is not an answer in itself to the question of how to make the most of your life. And the devirusing results apply only to the individual who spends decades following the discipline, not to society as a whole, and you still have to live there. It's no wonder that so many stories of Zen monks end with them

---

*For a wonderful do-it-yourself course in Zen koans, see Thomas Cleary's translation of the best-known collection of koans, entitled *No Barrier* (Bantam Books, 1993).

moving to the top of a mountain or under a bridge to spend the rest of their days in solitude. Once you clear your mind, it's easy to form the opinion that the rest of the world is running around aimlessly like headless chickens.

If you're wondering whether practicing Zen or simply becoming more aware of your thoughts would benefit you, here's an easy test: Can you easily turn off your internal conversation and just *be?* Try putting this book aside and not thinking any thoughts for the next minute. Do it now.

If you had difficulty doing that—if you kept talking to yourself inside your head, or thoughts kept creeping in and distracting you from simply perceiving the world around you at the present moment—chances are you'd gain a valuable skill by practicing noticing your thoughts. Next time you're bored and tempted to turn on the TV, try this instead, a nonmystical "meditation" technique that I've found useful: Just get comfortable and clear your mind of any thoughts. If they do creep in, don't react to them; just notice them and let them go. See if you can go for five full minutes, and then observe how you feel.

If you learn to turn off your internal dialogue, you've made the first big step toward freeing yourself from the tyranny of mind viruses. While you still may not fully realize which programs you're running because they support your purpose in life, and which you're running because you got infected with a virus of the mind, at least you know how to turn them off at will. Further, when you quiet your mind, you can make far better use of your intuition, which will lead you out of ruts and into places you may not have realized you wanted to go.

The Zen discipline goes beyond learning how to turn off your inner dialogue. The Zen student goes through life looking at events from a series of different perspectives given to her by her master in the form of koans.

> By looking at life from these different perspectives, the student eventually realizes that many of the beliefs she had taken for granted about the nature of reality were simply figments of her imagination.

This process, Zen adherents believe, eventually results in the dissolving of all artificial beliefs and an understanding of the world at a new level. While I haven't spent 20 years in a Zen monastery, it's fair to say that most of the major growth and learning I've experienced as an adult has been a result of looking at things from different perspectives and finding out I was wrong about one pig-headed belief or another. At that point, people come crawling out of the woodwork to pat me on the back and say how happy they are to see the change in me. "Why didn't you tell me about this before?" I ask. "We tried," comes the chorus of replies.

One useful way to try out flexing your point of view is to take advantage of any disagreement you have with anyone. Instead of trying to win the argument or backing off from the conflict, try as hard as you can to see things from the other person's point of view. You'll know you've succeeded when the person you were arguing with says, "Yes! That's exactly what I meant!" In fact, you may even find that all the other person wanted was to be understood.

Once you learn that new point of view, over the next several days try using it a few times to look at situations that come up. See how it feels. Even if you don't end up adopting it as your own belief, at least you'll understand how some other people react to things differently from you. That understanding will be valuable to you no matter what you want to do with your life.

> Most people are so full of mind viruses, of externally acquired mental programming, that they don't spend much of their time and energy pursuing what they want in life.

In fact, it's probably fair to say most people aren't even very clear about what they want in life. Noticing your thoughts and flexing your point of view are the best tools I know for understanding the difference between who you are and how you've been programmed. Try it—you'll like it!

The Learning Pyramid

Mind viruses take advantage of people's learning styles, or *heuristics*. By advancing the way you learn from the survival-and-reproduction heuristic you were born with, you can effectively immunize yourself against mind viruses.

You go through different levels of learning heuristics in your life, each building upon the previous in a kind of pyramid. Stepping from one level of the pyramid to the next requires not just learning a different subject, but jumping to a whole new manner of learning, and in fact a whole new way of looking at the world.

> People outgrow their belief systems, like butterflies leaving the cocoon.

Obviously, outgrowing a belief system doesn't mean the beliefs were wrong or bad. There's value in mastering one way of operating, getting so you can be that way with your eyes closed. We teach children about whole numbers and let them master that world before we start talking about fractions or real numbers. That doesn't mean integers are bad.

Outgrowing your belief system is more a transcendence than a repudiation. You'll still remember how to operate as you had before, but you'll realize that there's a bigger game available to play. As you'll see, the prize of the Level 3 game—living a free, purposeful, fulfilling, and meaningful life—is simply not available from Levels 1 or 2.

The first level of the pyramid is the genetic programming you were born with. This level was learned for you throughout the course of evolution; you don't need to do anything other than wander through life to get its benefits.

This level consists of the instinctual drives you and all animals have—remember the four *F*'s? This level lets you survive and reproduce in the world of nature. Through attraction and revulsion, through hunger, anger, fear, and lust, it's possible to survive with no further learning. All of traditional education, from nursery school through Ph.D. thesis, is designed to make the transition out of Level 1.

Some people stop here, never acquiring the self-discipline to master Level 2. Level 1 people lack foresight, self-discipline, and integrity. They tend to live chaotic lives, unable to hold a job or keep a relationship going. While they may enjoy the moments of life more than people in Level 2, they do not live powerfully.

If the four F's represented Level 1 of the learning pyramid, then the three R's characterize Level 2. All academic subjects, acquired skills, and fields of study make up Level 2. Reading, 'riting, and 'rithmetic—not to mention computer programming, political science, psychology, and religious doctrine—belong in this level.

Most people stop here. It takes so much work, so much time and effort, to acquire all the knowledge and beliefs that make up a healthy Level 2 that the task of transcending it all to make the jump to Level 3 seems not simply difficult but ridiculous. Beyond that, people who remember how much better life works in Level 2 than it did in Level 1 will be reluctant to give up the comfortable framework of the belief system that got them here.

> People who get stuck in Level 2 feel like they're in a rut or burned-out or that their lives lack meaning.

They become resigned or cynical. Often they are the ones who live Thoreau's "lives of quiet desperation." They may cling indefinitely to their religious beliefs, or to the currently popular anti-religious belief that life lacks meaning, hoping their faith in what they believe to be the Absolute Truth will eventually make things better. They may attempt to repeat past successes, go back to school, learn new subjects, or switch religions, but until they are willing to give up their reliance on the Truth of their belief systems, in Level 2 they will remain.

At this point, you may be wondering which level you're in. Again, most people are in Level 2. No one comes along and taps you on the shoulder saying it's time to move up to Level 3. In fact, you will have tremendous resistance to even considering that Level 3 exists or, if you acknowledge that it does, that you're not already in it. If you're living a life of quiet desperation, you're in Level 2. If you often feel bored, unmotivated, confused, resentful, guilty, unworthy, powerless, or like life lacks meaning, you're in Level 2. If you're just doing what you've always done without thinking much about what you want out of life, you're in Level 2 or 1.

I'm now going to say something about Level 3. If you're in Level 2, your first reaction will probably be to compare what I say to something you already know and form a conclusion about it. That is a Level 2 learning strategy that doesn't work in Level 3. I invite you to read with the possibility in mind that there's something here that's different from what you already know, and just kind of sit with that awhile.

Level 3 is learning to look at life as something to be *created* out of your personal programming and purpose—the two P's?— rather than as a maze of knowledge, beliefs, goals, and challenges to be run like a rat. It's complete personal freedom—freedom from societal pressures, freedom from guilt, freedom from mind viruses. (You know the trouble with the rat race, don't you? Even if you win, you're still a rat.)

In Level 3, you pick a purpose for your life and hold it as your highest priority. If you commit strongly enough to this purpose, the cognitive dissonance created with old memes that don't support this purpose will result in some reprogramming. After time, you'll find yourself becoming more and more effective at living your purpose. And again, I would recommend picking a purpose that you find rewarding, motivating, meaningful, and altogether fulfilling. You'll enjoy life and be good at what you do.

Spreading Memes to Others

If the purpose you pick involves influencing the lives of other people, you'll want to take up the second ethical question: *What memes do you want to spread?* As with the first question, there are many possible answers to this one.

One popular philosophy is *Live and let live.* I've got my beliefs, you've got yours, and that's fine. This is an offshoot of the *what comes naturally* strategy and as such, leaves evolution in the hands of selfish replicators that don't serve your quality of life. It's a very tempting position to take, almost a mandatory position for tolerant people in a free country. But there's a big difference between the government imposing totalitarian beliefs and individuals spreading memes they consider important. We've got to get over our distaste for evangelism if we want to have a positive impact on society; otherwise, mind viruses that make use of evangelism will win the battle for people's minds.

So, given that you can make a positive difference in people's lives by intentionally spreading memes, which memes will you spread? I leave that up to you. It shouldn't be hard for you, reading this book or *Getting Past OK,* to figure out that I'm in favor of people having a clear and accurate picture of the world and enjoying life. What kind of world would you like to live in? Go out and make it happen!

Regardless of whether you think it ethical to influence other adults' beliefs—to intentionally spread memes to other people— few would deny the value of influencing *children's* beliefs, of educating them. What new insights does memetics give us about childhood education? Can we use memetics to keep our kids from being harmfully infected by mind viruses, or to disinfect them once they are?

Disinfecting Our Children

One way to look at education is to see it as copying facts and ideas from the minds of one generation to the minds of the next. Copying memes. As such, education is subject to all the same invasions by viruses of the mind that the rest of society is prone to, and even more, since it is so intent on copying as its primary purpose.

The *tradition* meme dies hard in education. Is it any wonder our grade-school system is essentially the same structure invented by Plato more than 2,000 years ago? Is it a surprise that we still give students three months off in the summer long after it has ceased to be a practical requirement to tend the farm? Here's my favorite: despite decades of knowing that listening to lectures is perhaps the least effective way for people to learn, is it a shock that we still conduct classes primarily that way?

Is copying ideas and facts really the primary purpose of education, or should it be? Remember, without conscious effort on our parts, we tend to fall into the role of mind slaves of memes, living our lives to perpetuate and spread whatever memes are the most powerful.

> Can we consciously choose a better purpose for education than simply pumping our children's minds full of memes?

"You Have Not Yet Told Them What to Think!"

I remember a story my Russian-language teacher told me in high school. She said she had just returned from the *Soyuz Sovetskikh Sotsialisticheskikh Respublik*—Soviet Union, to you and me—where she had completed the second half of a teacher-exchange program. The classroom in Russia was almost entirely memorization and drills. The teacher would recite something, and the children would repeat it.

She said the Soviet teacher was befuddled by American teaching methods, in which students would be asked to discuss their thoughts on some subject the teacher brought up. "How can they discuss thoughts?" she puzzled. "You have not yet told them what to think!"

Her bemusement points out the major advance in education in the last century: a shift from memorization and skill sharpening to learning how to think. The "new math" of the '60s was designed to teach students to think abstractly about the entire system of mathematics rather than simply memorize methods and formulas. Once the students learned how to think in this one arena, it was hoped, they could apply this skill to the rest of their lives, turning into a generation of baby-boom Einsteins.

By my judgment, it worked, at least for the students who show up at school ready to learn. Educated young adults today are prepared to think abstractly about everything from politics to their own minds, creating a boom in the talk-show and mental-health industries. The shift in emphasis from *what to think* to *how to think*—along with such authority-shattering events as Vietnam and Watergate—has produced a generation of questioning minds. They question why things are the way they are, what their lives are about, what they should be. They are dissatisfied.

Reinventing Education

There's still a huge gap between what we teach children during those first 18 years and what it would be possible to teach them. Why don't we take advantage of those 18 years? What should we be teaching them instead? And who gets to decide?

The disappointing answer to the first question, why things are the way they are, is largely the subject of this book. Society, culture, power structures—it's difficult to make sense of any of them because they are the results of meme evolution, not anything designed by humankind for our own benefit. But suppose we could invent any education we wanted for our children. What would it be?

Imagine you're in charge of creating a brand-new society. You've got a school full of eager teachers and bright-eyed children just starting first grade. It's your job to decide what to do with those children for the next 12 years in order to give your society the best chance of flourishing and give *them* the best chance of having rich, full lives. What would you do?

The problem with our current educational system is that we don't ask questions like that very often, and when we do, any proposals that would call for substantial changes get hammered down by the entrenched power structure and by people's fear of change. We know something is wrong. Current talk about self-esteem in the classroom and outcome-based education proves that at least somebody's thinking about the problem.

The continued flight from the public schools by anyone who can afford it, the increasing popularity of homeschooling, and the steady decline in national test scores are all alarms sounding the immediacy and severity of our educational crisis. But how do we fix it? And if we figure out how to fix it, how do we convince the people in charge to actually do it?

What's Most Important?

Quick: start the clock! You've just been born. You've got exactly one lifetime to learn everything you need to know in order to live life, then live it. Ready? *Go!*

What kinds of things do you learn? Languages? The world capitals? Math? Music appreciation? Whatever it is, you'll need to learn everything other than what you got from your genes in this one lifetime. Sorry, no carryovers allowed. If you believe in such things, you can see a channeler or a psychic and get some tidbits from past lives, but that takes your time and energy just like any other form of learning.

With 1.4 million books in print, not to mention the out-of-print volumes in libraries and the 100,000 or so new ones coming out each year, you won't have time to read them all. How will you pick and choose?

There are five billion or so people on the planet with you. Who will you talk to, watch, learn from? Where will you go to school? What subjects will you take? Which assignments will you do, and which will you blow off in favor of hanging out in coffee-houses, getting drunk at parties, or other of life's nonacademic lessons? Whom will you have relationships with? Remember, marriage is the world's best (and frequently most expensive) personal-growth workshop. But there's only enough time to learn from a few people. Choose, quick!

Thanks to genetic evolution, along with modern advances in medicine and technology, you're born pretty much set to survive in the physical world. But the world of the mind, of society and culture, is a different story. You've got to learn just about everything starting with page one from the time you're born. And if you don't, you just kind of survive—and maybe never even know the difference, never know what you could have had, what life might have been like. Sad but true.

I hear a lot of talk about the failings of our educational system. Often critics compare our system unfavorably to that of Japan, where children go to school for many more hours and days than they do here. Their point is usually that as a result of the more intense education in Japan, children grow up to be better and more productive workers. Is growing up to be a better and more productive worker the point of education?

In my eyes, no. The point of education is to create a flourishing society in which as many people as possible have wonderful lives filled with freedom, happiness, and fulfillment. But not everyone would agree with me.

It's easy to find people and organizations willing to answer the other questions, about the meaning of life. The problem is, those answers are all either self-serving or part of some mind virus ready to hook you into a religious belief system. But the current fashion of eliminating any of these spiritual questions from school curricula creates a psychic hole in graduates, who within a few years begin to hunger for meaning in life.

Is it appropriate for school to teach students spiritual values? I don't think so, for a number of reasons. In the first place, *power* corrupts. Anyone or any group who got the charter to decide what values to teach would quickly become infected with every tricky and pernicious mind virus in existence, not to mention some new ones that would evolve just for the occasion. That's the primary benefit of our separation of church and state.

Maybe the solution is a separation of school and state. Is it time to give up on the idea of public schools, throw in the towel, and admit it just can't work? Maybe central schooling, a cultural

institution with a great concentration of power, is just too susceptible to virus infection. In the abstract, it's an attractive idea to
eliminate public schools and throw the school doors wide open to
competition.

Who Gets to Decide?

Who gets to decide? Who gets to control that initial programming we give our children before we kick them out of the nest
and let them fly on their own? Right now it's pretty haphazard.
In fact, the schools are so weak today that kids get much of their
programming from television. We're not making much of a conscious effort to direct our children's lives in school anymore. Many
overworked teachers complain they're the only ones who are trying, and the job is just too big. As a result we see children without
a strong family life being swept up in an explosion of youth-
oriented subcultures with powerful memes: gangs.

Saying it's the parents' job to supply the children with values
and direction won't work for these kids who don't have much of a
family. The schools are the place to start tapping these kids' interests and showing them there is indeed an opportunity for them to
have a great life.

The Next Great Shift

Whatever the method, the next great shift in education needs
to be as big a shift as the movement from memorization to learning how to think. The next step in education is teaching children
to decide for themselves what is most important in their lives—
facilitating their leap to Level 3 of the learning pyramid.

That means empowering them to discover what excites
them, motivates them, makes them feel worthy (you know, "self-
esteem"), and gives life meaning for them. It means telling them
the purpose of their lives is to make the most of these things, not

to be a cog in the self-perpetuating mechanism of random culture. It goes beyond handing out buttons telling them to "question authority" or bumper stickers exhorting them to "subvert the dominant paradigm," and giving them license to be their own authority and create their own paradigm. It means teaching them to be conscious! Conscious! Conscious! Conscious!

Scary? You bet. But the only way to wrest the course of our evolution away from the random selective forces of memes and get it in the hands of individuals is to be absolutely unwavering in our belief that each individual is entitled to life, liberty, and the pursuit of happiness. Right now all we're teaching kids is the pursuit of grades and approval. The pursuit of approval is an engraved invitation to the Viruses' Ball. It sucks you into whatever powerful mind virus pushes the most of your buttons. Children must be taught to discern and pursue their own values.

It's going to be a huge task to come up with a great curriculum that really works to program *all* children for a life of freedom and happiness, not slavery or despair. It's an even bigger task to sell it to the schools and get it up and running. It seems almost impossible, but what else is there to do? I've taken a baby step toward that goal by writing these words. The rest is up to you. And work fast. This one really is a crisis.

RECOMMENDED READING

Evolution

Dawkins, Richard. *The Blind Watchmaker* (Norton, 1986). A convincing argument for evolution of species by natural selection, including merciless attacks on creationists and other non-Darwinian heretics.

Dawkins, Richard. *River Out of Eden: A Darwinian View of Life* (Basic Books, 1995). The executive summary of the state of the art in evolutionary biology. If you've only got a couple of hours to learn about evolution, this is the book to read.

Dawkins, Richard. *The Selfish Gene, New Edition* (Oxford University Press, 1989). Brilliant explanation of the selfish-gene concept. The first book to describe the concept of the meme.

Dennett, Daniel C. *Darwin's Dangerous Idea: Evolution and the Meanings of Life* (Simon & Schuster, 1995). A lucid, thorough, and brilliant exploration of universal Darwinism: how evolution by natural selection can and does apply to all aspects of the universe.

Plotkin, Henry. *Darwin Machines and the Nature of Knowledge* (Harvard University Press, 1993). Meaty and intellectual exploration of the evolutionary basis of knowledge and learning, a subject known as *evolutionary epistemology.*

Computer Evolution

Levy, Steven. *Artificial Life* (Vintage Books, 1992). Fascinating roundup of the state of the art in this new field of computer science.

Evolution of Memes

Csikszentmihalyi, Mihaly. *The Evolving Self* (HarperCollins, 1993). Thoughts on the future as seen through the theory of memetic evolution.

Evolutionary Psychology

Buss, David M. *The Evolution of Desire* (Basic Books, 1994). A clear exposition of the mating-strategy aspect of evolutionary psychology, backed up by impressive academic studies.

Dennett, Daniel C. *Consciousness Explained* (Little, Brown, 1991). A masterwork about the nature of human thought with an excellent section on memes.

Wright, Robert. *The Moral Animal: Why We Are the Way We Are: The New Science of Evolutionary Psychology* (Pantheon, 1994). Incisive examination of the divergent evolution of male and female mating strategies, combined with a biography of Darwin.

Men's and Women's Roles

Gray, John. *Men are from Mars, Women are from Venus* (Harper-Collins, 1992). A practical, straightforward book explaining the differences in men's and women's needs and communication styles in relationships.

Cultural Viruses

Bulgatz, Joseph. *Ponzi Schemes, Invaders from Mars, & More Extraordinary Popular Delusions and the Madness of Crowds* (Harmony Books, 1992). Amazing stories of historical mind viruses. The one thing we learn from history is that we don't learn from history.

Rushkoff, Douglas. *Media Virus!* (Ballantine Books, 1994). Interesting exploration of the evolution of television and speculation on the use of Trojan horses to bundle hidden agendas with palatable memes.

Cults and Programming

Cialdini, Robert B. *Influence: The Psychology of Persuasion, Revised Edition* (Quill, 1993). Mind-boggling, easy-to-read book about psychological techniques being used every day to influence people's minds. If you liked Chapter 8, you'll love this book.

McWilliams, Peter. *Life 102: What to Do When Your Guru Sues You* (Prelude Press, 1994). The author of several best-selling self-improvement books recounts the events that led to his being brainwashed into spending 15 years in and giving $1 million to a cult.

Zen

Cleary, Thomas. *No Barrier: Unlocking the Zen Koan* (Bantam, 1993). Superb explanation of Zen introduces a brilliant translation of the *Wumenguan,* the most famous book of Zen riddle-lessons.

Hofstadter, Douglas R. *Gödel, Escher, Bach: An Eternal Golden Braid* (Vintage, 1979). Even though Thomas Cleary claims Hofstadter doesn't really grok Zen, any serious student of the nature of the mind should read this Pulitzer Prize–winning labor of love.

Pirsig, Robert M. *Zen and the Art of Motorcycle Maintenance* (Bantam, 1974). Autobiographical narrative of the author's inquiry into the nature of reality, distinctions, and sanity. Starts like a travelogue, but takes a sharp turn into the philosophical in Chapter 6.

Life Purpose

Brodie, Richard. *Getting Past OK: A Straightforward Guide to Having a Fantastic Life* (Warner Books, 1995). How to use the art of mental reprogramming to transform your quality of life, told through the author's personal life experiences and illustrated with Eggbert cartoons.

Frankl, Viktor. *Man's Search for Meaning* (Washington Square Press, 1984). Moving, thoughtful, and persuasive argument for having a life purpose, told through firsthand accounts of life in Nazi death camps.

Maslow, A. H. *The Farther Reaches of Human Nature* (Penguin, 1971). Very difficult reading about the nature of self-actualization and higher human values, but if you like authoritative credentials, you can't get much better than Maslow's.

ACKNOWLEDGMENTS

Susan Goplen, Greg Kusnick, Bill Marklyn, and Steven Salta each devoted an extraordinary amount of time and thought to assisting me with the shape and content of *Virus of the Mind*. Their support shows up not only in the ideas they contributed, but in their enthusiasm for my getting the book out there.

Marc de Hingh, Bob Matthews, and Lloyd Sieden all gave me detailed feedback on the manuscript, yielding many improvements in clarity. I rewrote entire chapters based on some of their lucid questions and criticisms.

George Atherton, Jon Bazemore, Robin Burchett, Dan Dennett, Ashton MacAndrews, Holly Marklyn, Elan Moritz, Richard Pocklington, Peter Rinearson, Matthew Senft, Charles Simonyi, Brett Thomas, and Eric Zinda all took time from their busy schedules to comment on the manuscript. Each one's contribution shows up in at least one improvement to the book's content.

My brother Mike Brodie swooped in from Southeast Asia just in time for last-minute proofreading and moral support.

Liz Greene helped me proof the current edition.

Finally, thanks to Richard Dawkins for being so gracious when he discovered I had inadvertently "pinched" the title he had previously used in an essay ("Viruses of the Mind").

My genes thank you. My memes thank you. My viruses of the mind thank you. And I thank you.

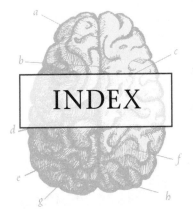

INDEX

A page number in *italics* indicates an illustration on that page.

ABOUT THE AUTHOR

Richard Brodie is best known as the original author of Microsoft Word. His self-help book, *Getting Past OK,* is an international bestseller. Richard has appeared on dozens of television and radio shows, including *The Oprah Winfrey Show.*

Richard continues to pursue wide and varied interests, which he occasionally blogs about at: **www.liontales.com**.

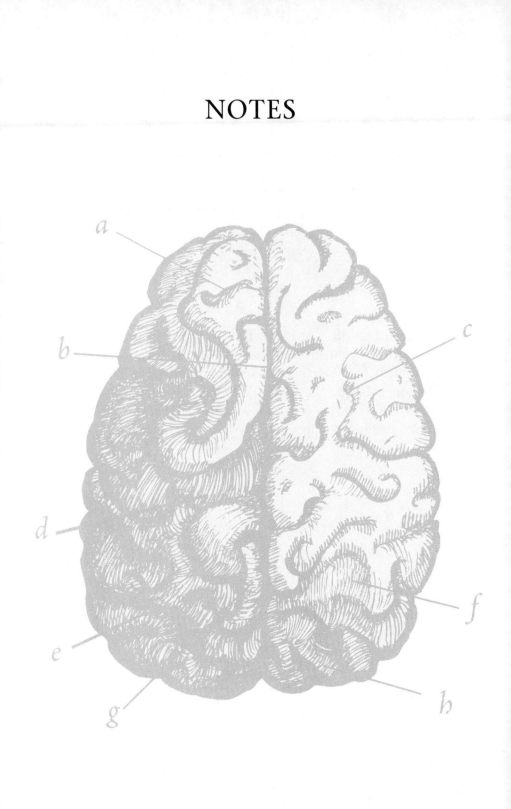

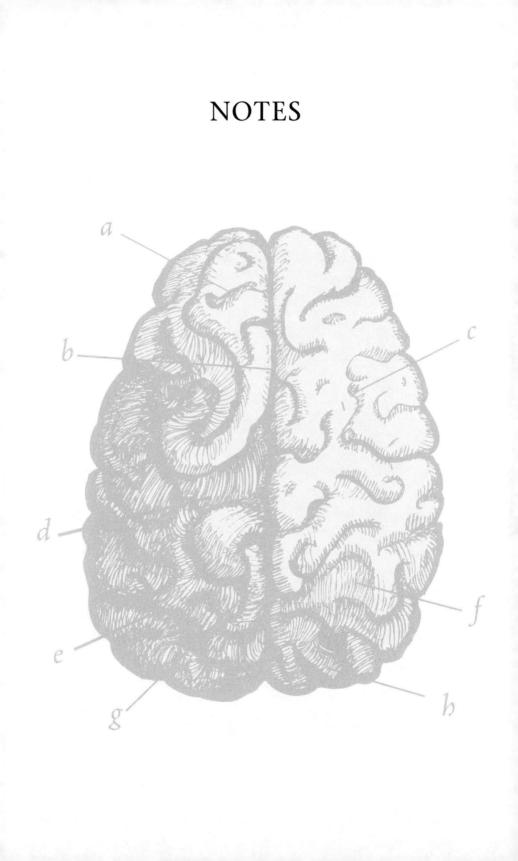

NOTES

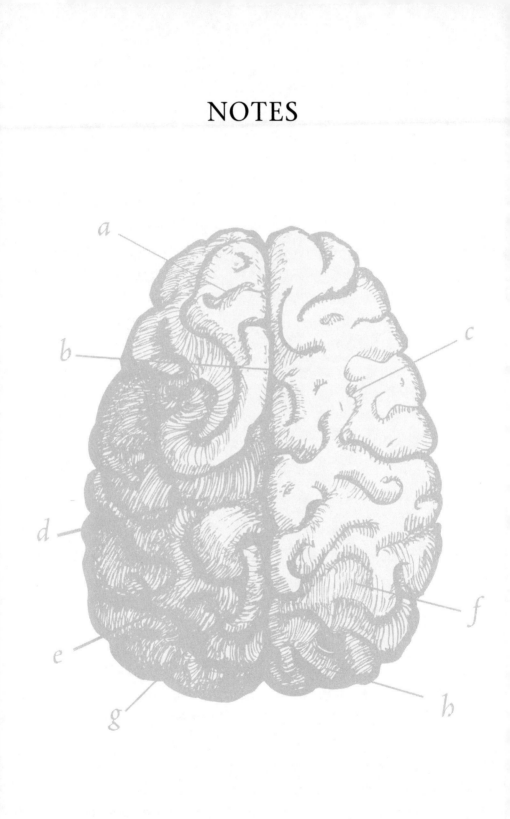

NOTES

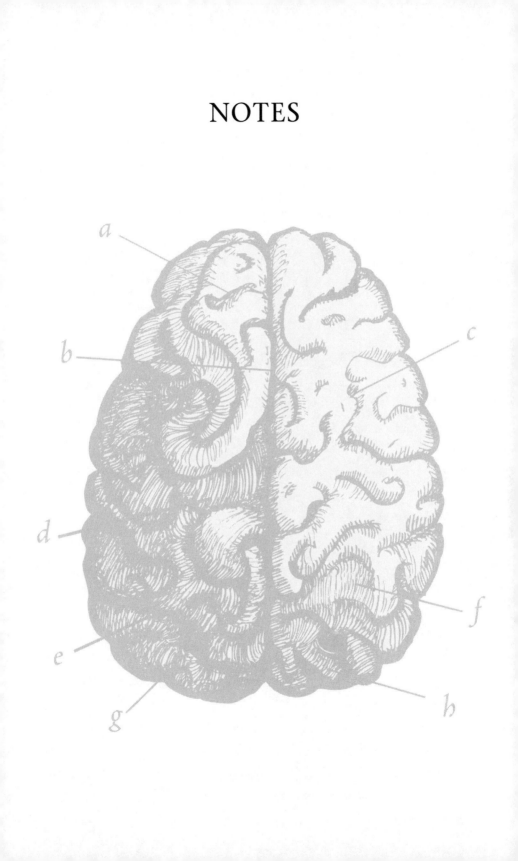

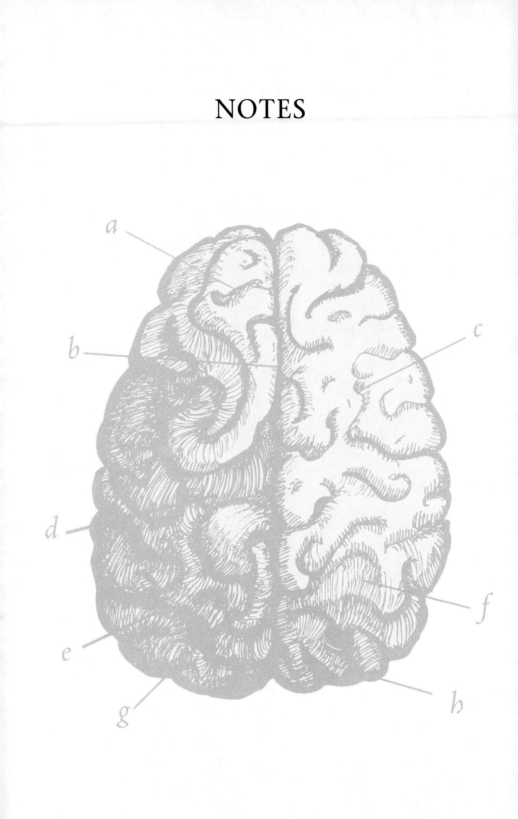

NOTES

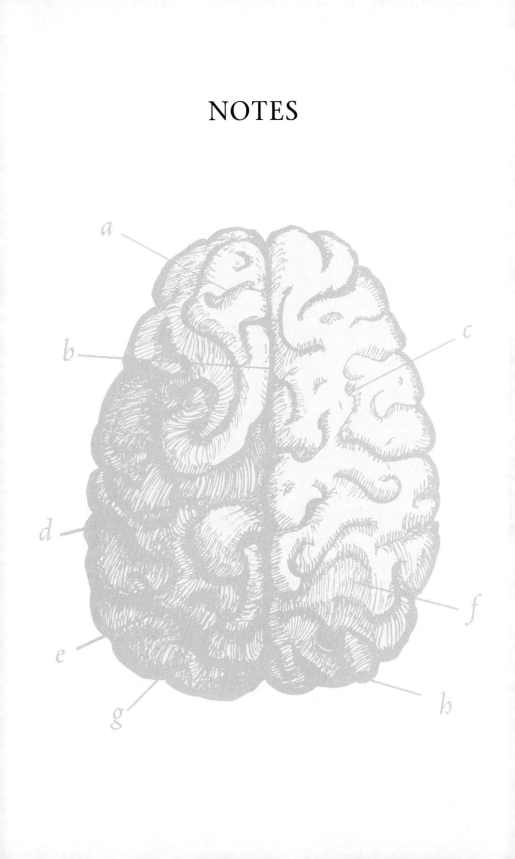

NOTES

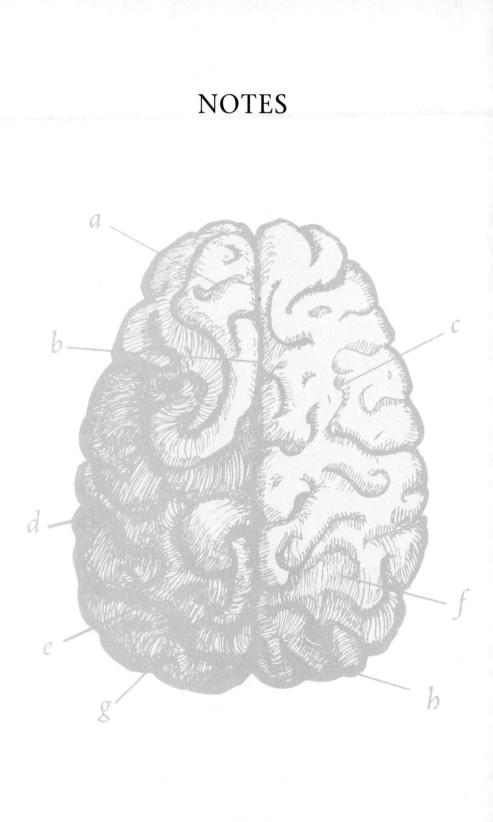

NOTES

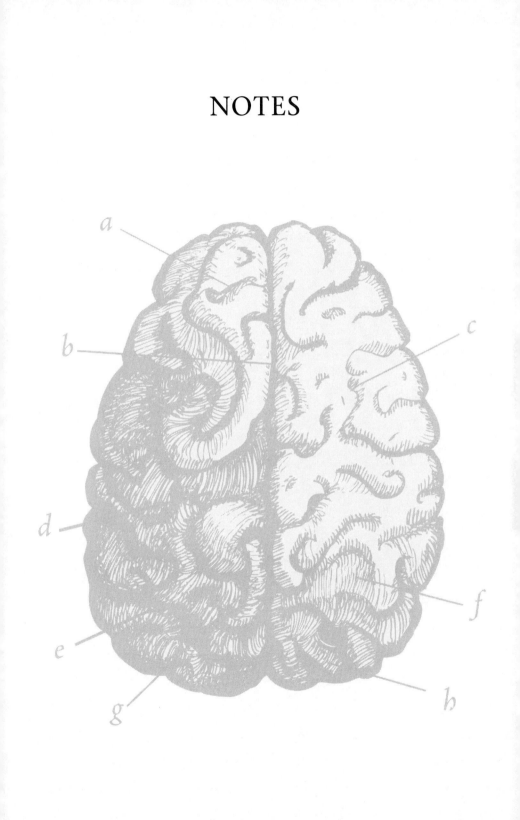

NOTES

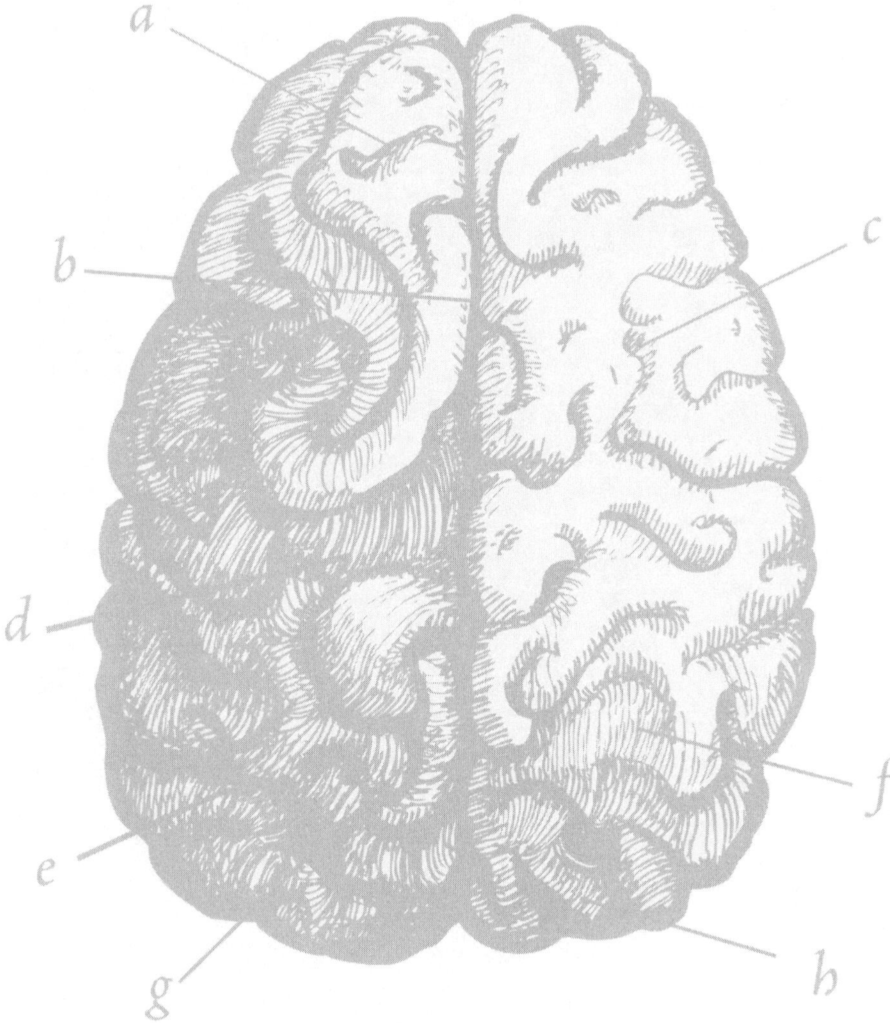

NOTES

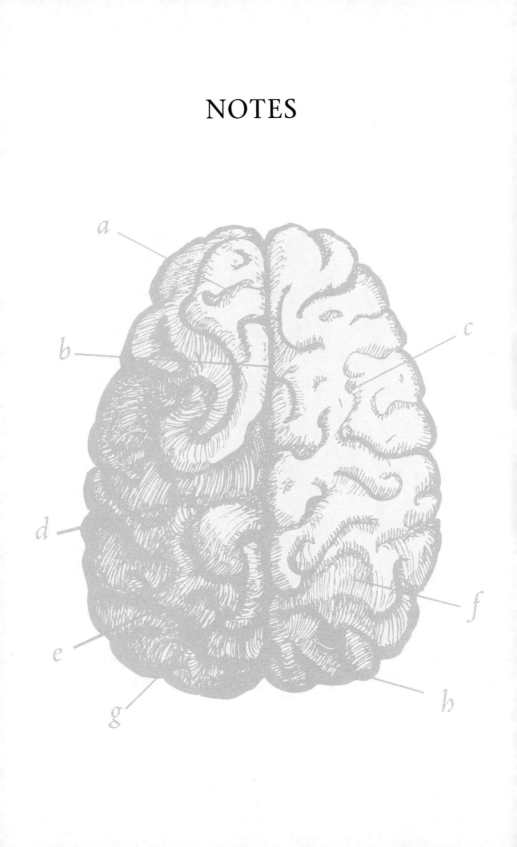

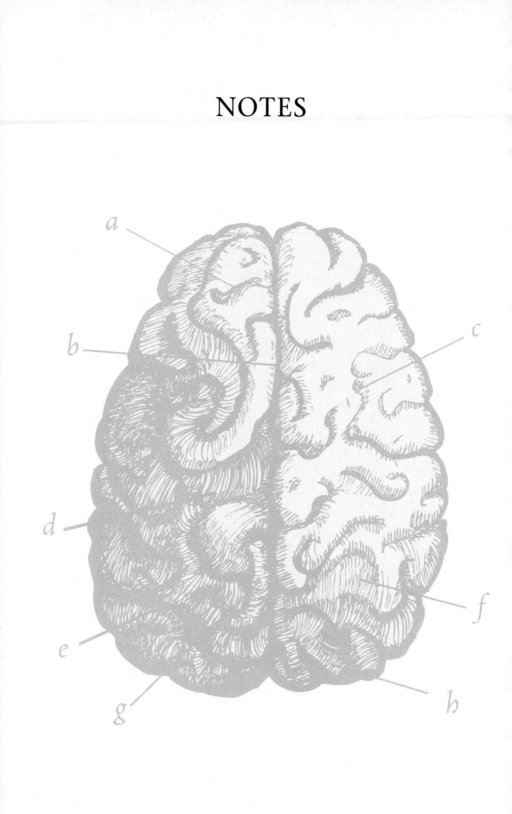

NOTES

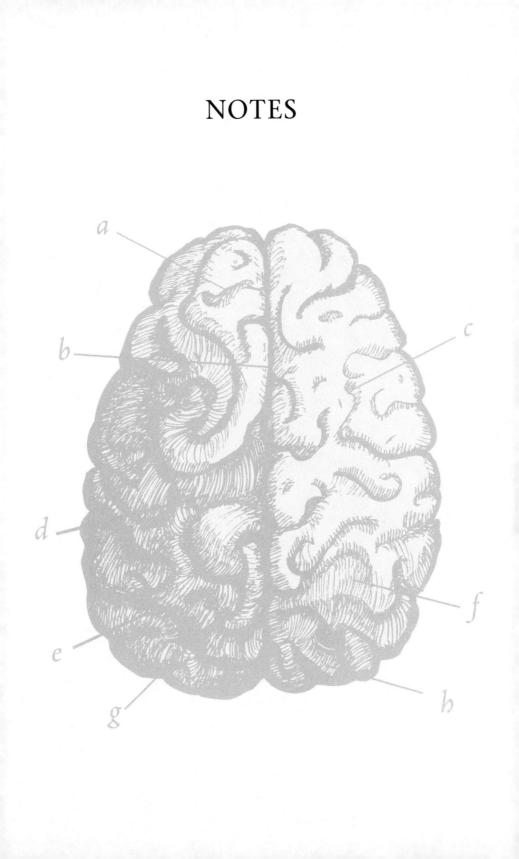

We hope you enjoyed this Hay House book.
If you'd like to receive our online catalog featuring additional
information on Hay House books and products, or
if you'd like information about the Hay Foundation, please contact:

Hay House, Inc.
P.O. Box 5100
Carlsbad, CA 92018-5100

(760) 431-7695 or (800) 654-5126
(760) 431-6948 (fax) or (800) 650-5115 (fax)
www.hayhouse.com® • www.hayfoundation.org

Published and distributed in Australia by: Hay House Australia
Pty. Ltd., 18/36 Ralph St., Alexandria NSW 2015 • *Phone:*
612-9669-4299 • *Fax:* 612-9669-4144 • www.hayhouse.com.au

Published and distributed in the United Kingdom by: Hay House UK,
Ltd., 292B Kensal Rd., London W10 5BE • *Phone:* 44-20-8962-1230
Fax: 44-20-8962-1239 • www.hayhouse.co.uk

Published and distributed in the Republic of South Africa by:
Hay House SA (Pty), Ltd., P.O. Box 990, Witkoppen 2068 • *Phone/Fax:*
27-11-467-8904 • orders@psdprom.co.za • www.hayhouse.co.za

Published in India by: Hay House Publishers India, Muskaan
Complex, Plot No. 3, B-2, Vasant Kunj, New Delhi 110 070 • *Phone:*
91-11-4176-1620 • *Fax:* 91-11-4176-1630 • www.hayhouse.co.in

Distributed in Canada by: Raincoast, 9050 Shaughnessy St.,
Vancouver, B.C. V6P 6E5 • *Phone:* (604) 323-7100
Fax: (604) 323-2600 • www.raincoast.com

Take Your Soul on a Vacation

Visit **www.YouCanHealYourLife.com®** to regroup, recharge, and
reconnect with your own magnificence.
Featuring blogs, mind-body-spirit news, and life-changing wisdom from
Louise Hay and friends.

Visit **www.YouCanHealYourLife.com** today!